The States in West German Federalism

THE STATES IN WEST
GERMAN FEDERALISM

A Study of Federal-State Relations, 1949-1960

BY

ROGER HEWES WELLS

Professor of Political Science
Bryn Mawr College

BOOKMAN ASSOCIATES

New York

MANUFACTURED IN THE UNITED STATES OF AMERICA BY
UNITED PRINTING SERVICES, INC.
NEW HAVEN, CONN.

TO
Stella Dueringer Wells

PREFACE

Since World War II, renewed attention has been given to federalism as a pattern for national, regional, and international organization. The evidence of such interest is widespread: the Commission on Intergovernmental Relations in the United States; the federal constitutions and constitutional proposals within the Commonwealth of Nations, notably in India, Malaya, the British Caribbean area, and Africa; likewise in Africa, the stimulus given to federalism in the Community under the Constitution of the Fifth French Republic; the problem of the Congo released from Belgian rule; and the regional developments in Western Europe represented by the Coal and Steel Community, the Common Market and EURATOM, which may eventually lead to a United States of Europe. On the supra-regional scale, world federalism and Atlantic Union have been advocated in spite of the serious obstacles to their realization. To this list must be added the Federal Republic of Germany, established in 1949.

Although German federalism has a long history, its annals and theories from the Middle Ages to the destruction of the Weimar Republic by Hitler are not set forth here. They are treated elsewhere, for example, in Ellinor von Puttkamer, ed., *Föderative Elemente im deutschen Staatsrecht seit 1648* (Göttingen, 1955) ; Arnold Brecht, *Federalism and Regionalism in Germany: The Division of Prussia* (New York, 1945) ; and Rupert Emerson, *State and Sovereignty in Modern Germany* (New York, 1928), chaps. 3 and 6. Attention is concentrated on the period since the overthrow of the National Socialist regime in 1945, especially the years since the founding of the Federal Republic.

As a problem of intergovernmental relations, West German federalism may be examined from either the federal or the state level. The latter approach is stressed in the following pages. No attempt is made to cover all aspects of federal politics, legislation, and administration, and the same is true of local government. The crux of federalism is federal-state relations, which is one of the two major emphases in this analysis. The other emphasis seeks to give a brief but clear picture of government in the states or "Länder" as they are called. At appropriate points, comparisons are made between the United States and the "Bundesrepublik Deutschland." Except incidentally, the postwar policies of the Allies in Germany are not discussed; these are examined in Harold Zink, *The United States in Germany, 1944-1955* (Princeton, 1957) ; and in Eugene Davidson, *The Death and Life of Germany: An Account of the American Occupation* (New York, 1959) .

There is a large body of published materials on West Germany. See John Brown Mason, "Government, Administration and Politics in West Germany: A Selected Bibliography," *American Political Science Review,* vol. 52 (1958) , pp. 513-530; and Roger H. Wells' bibliography on German state and local government, *ibid.,* vol. 50 (1956) , pp. 1112-1115. Mason has also prepared a bibliography on East Germany, *ibid.,* vol. 53 (1959) , pp. 507-523.

Many German words, such as Bund, Bundesrepublik, Bundestag, Bundesrat, Land and Landtag, are commonly used and understood in English without being translated. These are not italicized in the text as is done with less familiar terms, such as *Grundgesetz, Verfassung, Gemeinde* and *Landkreis.* In the notes, no German words are italicized except in titles of books and periodicals.

While the author has drawn upon his observations, interviews and experiences in Germany (both as a private citizen and as a staff member of the Office of Military Government for Germany (US) and of the Office of the U.S. High Commissioner for Germany), his debt to those who have written about West Germany is great. Special thanks are due to his Bryn Mawr colleagues, Professors Myra R. Jessen and Hertha Kraus, and to Mr. John G. Kormann of the U.S. Department of State for reading all or parts of the manuscript and for making valuable criticisms and suggestions, most of which have been incorporated in the final version expertly typed by Mrs. Eric D. Blanchard. However, the author assumes sole responsibility for the study.

R.H.W.

Bryn Mawr, Pennsylvania
August, 1960

CONTENTS

The States in West German Federalism

1 STATE TERRITORIAL ORGANIZATION

The study of West German state government may properly
begin with territorial organization. The "Bundesrepublik
Deutschland," with its ten Länder, is less than half the size
of the Reich created by Bismarck in the nineteenth century.
Prior to the Bismarckian unification, it was customary to
speak of the "the Germanies." Today the term has again
become current; the Federal Republic is one Germany
among several.

THE OTHER GERMANIES

By the "other Germanies," Germans usually mean the lost
Prussian provinces, East Germany, and Berlin. Important
and controversial as these are, they can only be briefly
mentioned here. As a result of World War II, the territories
east of the Oder-Neisse Line have come under direct Polish
or Soviet control. Their return to German jurisdiction in
the near future is unlikely. The remainder of the eastern
part of the country, except Berlin, constituted the original
Soviet zone of occupation. It has become a firmly held
Communist satellite officially dubbed the "Deutsche De-
mokratische Republik." In view of the prolonged deadlock
on German reunification, it is improbable that the two

German republics will soon be joined, either in a federal scheme favored by the West or in a "confederation" sponsored by the East.

The course of state government in the German Democratic Republic has been far different from that in the Bundesrepublik. Early in the occupation, the Soviet military government created five Länder—Brandenburg, Mecklenburg, Saxony, Saxony-Anhalt, and Thuringia. Each was provided, at least on paper, with its own state constitution and governmental organs. So far as area, population, and resources were concerned, they were all potentially satisfactory units of a united federal Germany. Instead, the whole trend in East Germany has been toward a highly centralized, Communist-dominated regime. In 1952, the Länder themselves were abolished and replaced by fourteen districts (*Bezirke*).

At the center of the German Democratic Republic, 110 miles from the nearest point in the Federal Republic, is the city of Berlin, the historic capital of the united Reich. Like the country as a whole, it is split between East and West. East Berlin is the capital of East Germany and has its own city government.

The heroic story of West Berlin has often been told. Constantly threatened and harassed, the subject of interminable negotiations between the Soviet Union and the West, it continues to stand as a beacon of freedom. West Berlin is a state (Land) as well as a city and thus resembles the city-states of Bremen and Hamburg.[1] It is in effect, although not in law, the eleventh state of the Bundesrepublik.[2] For all practical purposes, "Free Berlin" functions as if it were a part of the Federal Republic, from which it receives substantial financial and economic assistance.[3] However, there are so many peculiarities in its status that it is not dealt with in the present study.

THE WEST GERMAN STATES

The Federal Republic consists of the following states (Länder) .[4]

State	Capital	Area (Sq. miles)	Population (January 1, 1959)
Baden-Württemberg	Stuttgart	13,803	7,433,000
Bavaria	Munich	27,239	9,278,000
Bremen	Bremen	156	677,500
Hamburg	Hamburg	288	1,807,600
Hesse	Wiesbaden	8,150	4,651,500
Lower Saxony	Hanover	18,284	6,515,600
North Rhine–Westphalia	Düsseldorf	13,111	15,459,300
Rhineland-Palatinate	Mainz	7,656	3,354,700
Saar	Saarbrücken	991	1,040,100
Schleswig-Holstein	Kiel	6,054	2,275,800

Except for the Saar and Baden-Württemberg, the existing states were all established or confirmed by the Allied military governments prior to the launching of the Federal Republic in 1949.[5] Some of them, such as Bavaria and the Hanseatic city-states of Bremen and Hamburg, are historic units, more ancient than the Commonwealths of Virginia and Massachusetts. The Bavarian Constitution proudly recalls that that Land has had "more than a thousand years of history."

Other Länder were formed in whole or in part from territories of the state of Prussia, which was never reconstituted after the war and was officially declared abolished by the occupying powers in 1947. Schleswig-Holstein is the former Prussian province by that name, to which the city-state of Lübeck, and Eutin from Land Oldenburg were added by the Hitler regime in 1937. Lower Saxony is chiefly the Prussian province of Hanover plus the former states of Brunswick, Oldenburg, and Schaumburg-Lippe. North Rhine–Westphalia combines the Prussian province of Westphalia, the northern part of the Prussian Rhine province and the state of Lippe. Hesse is an amalgamation of most of the old Land Hesse and of the Prussian province of Hesse-Nassau. Possibly the greatest conglomeration is Rhineland-Palatinate which was pieced together from Prussian, Hessian, and Bavarian (the Bavarian Palatinate) fragments.

The two most recent Bundesländer are the Saar (1957) and Baden-Württemberg (1952). The Saar, with its important coal resources, was long a pawn in the struggles between France and Germany.[6] From 1815 to 1919, the territory was German. Then for fifteen years (1920-1935), it was under the League of Nations until the plebiscite of 1935 returned it to Germany.

After World War II, the Saar was originally a part of the French zone of occupation. However, it was soon given a special status which brought economic union with France and a quasi-autonomous political regime. It figured prominently in the larger questions of Franco-German relations involving the European Coal and Steel Company (1952), the rejected European Defense Community, and the Western European Union (1954). On October 23, 1955, the voters of the area decisively rejected the proposal to give the Saar a kind of European status under the Western European Union. Further negotiations resulted in a series of agreements (1956) transferring the Saar to Germany.[7]

On January 1, 1957, the territory became the tenth Land of the Federal Republic. However, since full economic union, as contrasted with political incorporation, required further legal and economic adjustments, a transitional period was provided. Economic union was not formally completed until July 6, 1959.

BADEN-WUERTTEMBERG: ONE STATE OR TWO?

The Baden-Württemberg question has been the subject of litigation before the Federal Constitutional Court (*Bundesverfassungsgericht*). When the occupation zones were established in 1945, the historic states of Baden and Württemberg were divided. The United States, having received North Baden and North Württemberg, soon combined them into a single Land, Württemberg-Baden. South Baden and South Württemberg were assigned to the French zone and each was made into a separate Land by military government. South Württemberg was known as Württemberg-Hohenzollern because the Prussian enclave of Hohenzollern was incorporated into it.

The resulting map was highly unsatisfactory to all parties concerned. The French pressed for the whole of Baden which thus might become a kind of buffer state for France. For logistic and diplomatic reasons, the United States was unwilling to exchange North Baden for South Württemberg.[8] The Germans objected to the hardships of the artificial zonal frontier. The union of North Baden and North Württemberg ran counter to the fact that Baden had been traditionally Catholic while Württemberg was Protestant. Particularism in North Baden also showed itself in dislike at being "annexed" and governed from Stuttgart, the capital of the old state of Württemberg.

From 1948 onward, the territorial reorganization of Southwest Germany was much discussed. Should there be a single "Southwest State" made up of Baden and Württemberg, or should Land Baden and Land Württemberg be restored as they were before 1945 (the objective desired by the "*Altbadener*" organized into the *Heimatbund Badenerland*)? The good results of the union of North Baden and North Württemberg argued for the larger state which would thus be a strong constituent unit of the Federal Republic.

During the military government period (1945-1949), it was not possible to secure agreement on a definitive reorganization of the West German Länder in general and of the Southwest region in particular. Hence the Constitution (*Grundgesetz*) [9] of the Bundesrepublik, framed and adopted in the city of Bonn which thereupon became the federal capital, went into effect in September 1949 with the eleven existing states.

Article 29 of that document, which will be subsequently examined, contains the general principles and procedures for territorial reorganization. Article 118, a transitional provision, states:

> Notwithstanding the provisions of Article 29, the reorganization of the territory comprising the states of Baden, Württemberg-Baden and Württemberg-Hohenzollern may be effected by agreement between the states concerned. If no agreement is reached, the reorganization will be regulated by a federal law which must provide for a referendum (*Volksbefragung*).

Since the three states disagreed, in May 1951 the Federal Parliament enacted legislation calling for a referendum on the formation of the Southwest State. If this were rejected by the electorate, the states of Baden and Württemberg would automatically be restored. In the referendum of December 9, 1951, almost 70 percent of those voting in the area as a whole favored the single Land.[10] The law further required that there must be majorities in three out of the four parts if the Southwest State were to be established. Such majorities were obtained in the two sections of Württemberg and in North Baden. However, in South Baden, 62 percent of those voting opposed the union. With this popular approval of the proposed new Land, the state of Baden-Württemberg was launched in 1952.

Prior to the referendum, the government of South Baden had challenged the legislation in the Federal Constitutional

Court. There were, in fact, two federal laws involved.[11] The first, the so-called *"Blitzgesetz,"* extended the terms of the South Baden and Württemberg-Hohenzollern legislatures until the expiration of their own constitutions following the reorganization of the Southwest region. The second provided for the referendum. On October 23, 1951, the Court declared the *Blitzgesetz* unconstitutional but upheld the referendum in its essentials.[12]

However, that was not the end of the story. As explained in the next section, a federal law was passed in December 1955 implementing Article 29 of the Constitution.[13] Under this statute, the *Heimatbund Badenerland* asked permission to launch an initiative petition (*Volksbegehren*) calling for a referendum in the former state of Baden. When this was refused by the Federal Minister of the Interior, on the ground that the territorial reorganization already carried out under Article 118 precluded resort to Article 29, an appeal was filed with the Federal Constitutional Court. On May 30, 1956, in two cases, the Court overruled the Minister of the Interior.[14] The *Heimatbund* was authorized to proceed with the initiative petition and did in fact secure the required number of signatures in October 1956.[15]

In both 1957 and 1958, a group of more than one hundred members of the Bundestag (the lower house of the Federal Parliament) introduced a bill calling for a referendum in the former Land Baden on the question of restoring that state.[16] The proposal was strongly opposed by the government of Baden-Württemberg which argued that the issue could not be settled by Baden alone but that Württemberg must also be heard.[17] The Bundestag's Committee on Law opposed the bill as unconstitutional. The Federal Minister of the Interior strongly objected to all territorial reorganization except in connection with the reunification of East and West Germany. Since that event is remote and the vested interests defending the existing Land boundaries are powerful, time works in favor of the continuance of Baden-Württemberg as it now is.[18]

While originally there was some criticism that Baden was unfairly treated in the distribution of state offices, Minister-President Kurt Georg Kiesinger, who took office in 1959, is from Baden. Moreover, the *Altbadener* have become weaker. In June 1959, they formed the "Christian" and "federal" *Badische Volkspartei* which in the following year combined with the *Deutsche Partei*. But in the Landtag election of May 15, 1960, the combination polled only 1.8 percent of the popular vote.[19]

TERRITORIAL REORGANIZATION UNDER ARTICLE 29

As previously indicated, a general territorial reorganization is envisaged by Article 29 of the West German Constitution, Section 1 of which reads:

> The federal territory shall be reorganized by federal law with due regard to regional ties, historical and cultural connections, economic stability and social structure. The reorganization should create states which by their size and capacity are able effectively to fulfill the functions incumbent upon them.

With reference to areas which, after May 8, 1945, had been incorporated into other states without a popular vote, Article 29 contained provisions for the use of the initiative and referendum. The initiative could be invoked within one year after the Constitution went into effect. However, in approving the Constitution, the three Western military governors made a reservation to Article 29. They declared that, except for Baden, Württemberg-Baden and Württemberg-Hohenzollern, the existing boundaries of the Länder must "remain as now fixed until the time of the peace treaty . . . unless the (Allied) High Commissioners should unanimously agree to change this position."[20] The result was to suspend all territorial reorganization except in Southwest Germany.

When the Federal Republic became a sovereign state in May 1955, the Allied reservation to Article 29 ceased to be operative. Even before that date, the implementation of Article 29 had received attention at Bonn. In January 1952, the Federal Cabinet appointed a committee of experts headed by former Chancellor Hans Luther, who had long been interested in the subject. After three years of study, the Luther Committee submitted its report examining the Länder in the light of the criteria laid down in Article 29.[21] It found that most of the states were going concerns, although the weakness of Schleswig-Holstein and Rhineland-Palatinate was noted. In Lower Saxony, there was some irredentist sentiment in the former Land Oldenburg, which, however, lacked the potential to be a viable separate state. The experts outlined possible territorial rearrangements but on the whole accepted the existing boundaries. Following the report, Parliament, on December 23, 1955, passed a law implementing Article 29.[22]

In accordance with this statute, initiative petitions were undertaken in areas which had been consolidated by military government fiat without a referendum.[23] In addition to Baden, discussed in the previous section, there were successful *Volksbegehren* in Oldenburg and Schaumburg-Lippe (state of Lower Saxony); and in Koblenz-Trier, Rhine-Hesse, and Montabaur (state of Rhineland-Palatinate). In the Palatinate (state of Rhineland-Palatinate), the *Volksbegehren* failed to secure the signatures of the required 10 percent of the voters.[24]

However, a successful initiative petition is not automatically followed by a referendum; there must first be additional federal legislation which has thus far not materialized. Because of the great opposition to further territorial reorganization within West Germany, this is unlikely to happen. [25]

COMPARISONS WITH THE UNITED STATES

Ideally under federalism, the constituent states should have adequate areas, populations, and resources and should not vary too much among themselves in these factors. Neither in the Federal Republic nor in the United States is this ideal realized. At one end of the scale, Bremen, Hamburg, and the Saar are each smaller in territory than is Rhode Island. At the other end, there is no longer the German equivalent of Texas, spreading over the map as Prussia once did. Bavaria, the largest Land, is bigger than West Virginia; while Lower Saxony, Baden-Württemberg, and North Rhine–Westphalia (ranking second, third and fourth, respectively) exceed Maryland in size. The areas of Hesse, Rhineland-Palatinate and Schleswig-Holstein are approximately the same as New Jersey.

With respect to the number of inhabitants, North Rhine–Westphalia, with about the same population as California, leads all the other states. In second place is Bavaria which is comparable with Ohio. Except for Bremen (which, nevertheless, is more populous than Delaware), the other Länder each have more than a million people.

Since World War II, there has been much discussion about the gap between the "advanced" and the "underdeveloped" countries of the world. A smaller but somewhat similar gap exists in the American and West German federal systems where some of the units are economically backward in comparison with the others.[26] There are wide differences in industrialization and wealth among the American states, and the same is true in the Federal Republic. Thus in 1959, Delaware stood first with a per capita personal income of

$2,946 while Mississippi, at the bottom, had only $1,162.[27] In the same fashion, one may contrast rich and urban North Rhine–Westphalia, which includes the Ruhr with its concentration of mines and heavy industries, and poor and rural Schleswig-Holstein. In 1955, the per capita personal income of the former was 3,223 DM and of the latter, 1,971 DM.[28] However, the general economic development and prosperity of the Federal Republic is lessening the economic differences between the Länder. On the other hand, for a number of years, the basic disparity was aggravated by the unequal distribution of refugees throughout the country with the result that the burden of caring for them fell more heavily on some states than on others. This important subject requires further explanation.[29]

The United States has had nothing comparable to the West German experience with expellees and refugees. After the Civil War, there was a veritable flood of immigrants, mostly from Europe. In the thirty-five years between 1880 and 1915, over 22,000,000 were admitted. From 1906 to 1915, there were six years when the influx exceeded one million people annually.[30] From the seventeenth century to the present, the Negroes have been a large, underprivileged minority. Today in various states, there is a serious social question centering around the migratory farm workers. But none of these phenomena developed in the same magnitude or as quickly as was the case in Europe where millions of people were uprooted during and after World War II.

The problem of integrating into West Germany ten million German expellees and refugees from the East,[31] which cast a dark shadow over the early postwar years, is steadily moving towards a solution. This is largely due to the Federal Government's vigorous program authorized under legislation such as the *Bundesvertriebenengesetz* of 1953[32] and the *Lastenausgleichgesetz* of 1952. Originally, there was an undue massing of these people in the agricultural areas of Schleswig-Holstein, Lower Saxony and Bavaria; there was little or no room for them in the bombed-out cities which, however, have since been rebuilt. This concentration has been reduced by resettlement in other parts of West Germany. Thus in the decade 1949-1959, 396,262 refugees were transferred from Schleswig-Holstein to other Länder, principally North Rhine–Westphalia and Baden-Württemberg.[33] On the other hand, refugees still number roughly one-third of the population in Schleswig-Holstein and Lower Saxony. It is not surprising that the Refugee Party developed political strength in these two states.

The map of Germany today is simple compared to what it was before the French Revolution when there were more than three hundred separate states of one sort or another.[34] Wholesale consolidations were made by Napoleon; these for the most part were confirmed by the Congress of Vienna which in 1815 united the surviving thirty-nine states in the German Confederation. During the next half century largely due to Bismarck's unifying efforts, the total was reduced to twenty-seven, all of which, except Austria and Liechtenstein, became members of the German Empire in 1871.

In the period of the Weimar Republic, further changes brought the number of Länder to seventeen, without, however, achieving the major objective of *Reichsreform,* namely, the division of giant Prussia. The National Socialist regime, while maintaining the territorial unity of Prussia, so merged it with the central government that the Prussian provinces became direct administrative subdivisions of the Reich.[35] After World War II, the reorganizations of the Allies were of decisive significance since they eliminated Prussia and most of the surviving dwarf Länder.

Thus the only major territorial changes since 1789 were those carried out by Napoleon, Bismarck, and the World

War II Allies. The territories of the Länder comprising the
Federal Republic are now more rationally organized than
ever before. Seen in retrospect after the dust has settled,
the post-1945 creation of Hesse, Lower Saxony, North
Rhine–Westphalia and Baden-Württemberg must be regarded as constructive solutions. Although small, the city-
states of Bremen and Hamburg have survived as separate
entities just as they did in previous German federalisms;
they seem to be as permanent as Bavaria. The Luther Committee was doubtful about Schleswig-Holstein but felt that
no change, such as union with Hamburg, was desirable.
The Committee was even more skeptical about that syn-
thetic creation, Rhineland-Palatinate. After a feeble start,
that Land is now more successful and has staunch defenders.
Its chances of survival appear better than when the Luther
Committee examined the question. As for the Saar, is has
so long been a special case that it shows little or no desire to
be united with any other state. In short, further state boundary changes are improbable before the reunification of East
and West Germany.

2 STATE GOVERNMENT AND POLITICS

The states in a federal system may be reasonably adequate in territorial area, population and resources, and yet fail as effective units. Other factors, such as governmental structure and politics, are also involved. While no constitution can guarantee that the desired results will be attained, unwise or obsolete provisions can be serious obstacles. The shortcomings of some American state governments are in part due to their archaic and wordy constitutions.

STATE CONSTITUTIONS

In the period 1946-1953, each of the West German Länder adopted a permanent democratic constitution (*Verfassung*).[1] These were usually enacted by the state legislature, but the constitutions of Baden-Württemberg, Bavaria, Hesse, and Rhineland-Palatinate were drafted by special constitutional conventions. In Bavaria, Bremen, Hesse, North Rhine–Westphalia, and Rhineland-Palatinate, the documents were ratified by popular referendum; in the others, they became operative without such action.[2]

The West German *Landesverfassungen* show considerable variation in methods of amendment, the most common requirement being a two-thirds vote of the Landtag. In Hamburg, Lower Saxony, the Saar, and Schleswig-Holstein, the state legislature alone has the power of amendment. In Bavaria and Hesse, amendments proposed by the Landtag must be ratified by popular referendum; in Bremen, Baden-Württemberg and North Rhine–Westphalia, there may be a referendum under certain circumstances. Bremen, North

Rhine–Westphalia and Rhineland-Palatinate permit the voters to initiate constitutional amendments.

Thus far, fewer than a score of amendments have been adopted in the ten states, most of which were not important.[3] For example, in 1950 the electorate of Hesse approved an amendment which authorized the Landtag to deviate from proportional representation in state and local election legislation (Articles 75, 137). A more controversial case occurred in Schleswig-Holstein. The Social Democratic majority in the Landtag had enacted the Constitution of 1949 without a popular referendum. The triumph of the opposition parties in the 1950 Landtag election resulted in the immediate adoption of two amendments by the new legislature. The first modified Article 6 on schools; the second struck out Article 8 on land reform.

The paucity of amendments is not due to difficult amending requirements such as put some American commonwealths in constitutional "strait-jackets." The reason lies elsewhere. Many American state constitutions are full of statutory materials which result in excessive length and make frequent changes necessary. The West German *Landesverfassungen* are largely confined to the "fundamentals" which do not call for frequent modification. Hence they possess brevity, a characteristic lacking in most American state constitutions.

The longest Land constitution is that of Bavaria, adopted in 1946. It has 188 articles[4] and contains approximately 9,000 words as compared with the 6,800 words in the Constitution of the United States and its 22 amendments. This contrasts with the Louisiana Constitution which has 201,000 words and with the much shorter Pennsylvania Constitution which still has 15,000 words.[5] Among the Länder, the Schleswig-Holstein Constitution is the shortest with 53 articles; indeed, it is too short to deal adequately with the fundamentals.

An important factor affecting the length of the state constitutions is the presence or absence of a bill of rights. The five *Landesverfassungen* adopted before the *Grundgesetz* (Bavaria, Bremen, Hesse, the Saar, Rhineland-Palatinate) have elaborate bills of rights. Of the five later constitutions, three (Hamburg, Lower Saxony, Schleswig-Holstein) have no bills of rights, doubtless on the theory that the *"Grundrechte"* of the Bonn Constitution make a separate state enumeration superfluous. The *Grundgesetz* declares (Articles 31, 142) that, although "Federal law overrides state law," the provisions of state constitutions which "guarantee basic rights in conformity with Articles 1 to 18 of this Basic Law also remains in force." The North Rhine–Westphalia Constitution of 1950 and the Baden-Württemberg Constitution of 1953 have state bills of rights; but they likewise adopt the Bonn basic rights by reference.[6]

Viewed as a whole, the West German state constitutions are both modern and adequate. They represent reasonable and workable compromises between the political parties and between the various organized groups within the society. While certain articles have been copied from the Constitution of the Weimar Republic and from the Land constitutions of the years 1919-1933,[7] the improvements made in the earlier patterns are significant. The postwar constitutional fathers, both federal and state, have profited from the shortcomings of the Weimar days and from the lessons of the Nazi tyranny.

Fundamental constitutional rights are better spelled out than before; and they are protected by judicial review,[8] by civil liberties organizations, and by the press and public opinion.[9] The problems of election methods and of cabinet stability have been grappled with, even if not with complete success, as the subsequent discussion will indicate. The control of emergency powers has been more carefully defined.[10]

PARTIES AND ELECTIONS

The Party System

State government structure cannot be discussed without first examining the political parties and the election laws under which the party system operates.[11] Although parties have great practical significance in the Länder, they have received almost no specific constitutional legitimation. While the Federal Constitution declares (Article 21) that "parties participate in forming the political will of the people,"[12] no such statement is found in the *Landesverfassungen*. (They do however, provide for the parliamentary form of government which assumes the existence of parties.) The word "Partei" does not occur in the state constitutions except that in Rhineland-Palatinate (Article 133) unconstitutional parties may be excluded from free elections. The omission is doubtless a reflection of the traditional hostility and suspicion toward parties, an attitude which is gradually being overcome in the postwar years as their role in a democracy is recognized.

Since 1945, the Christian Democrats (CDU) and the Social Democrats (SPD) have become the two major West German parties;[13] in the 1957 Bundestag election, their combined popular vote amounted to 82 percent of the valid ballots cast. It is probably still too early to say that the two-party system has fully arrived. According to Norbert Muhlen, the Federal Republic now has a "two-plus" party configuration, "a peculiar mixture of the plural-party system of continental European tradition and of the (American) two-party system."[14]

The CDU and the SPD are not the only nationwide parties. The Free Democratic Party (FDP) is national in character but is far weaker than its big rivals and has lost strength. The Refugee Party (GB-BHE)[15] has national aspirations, although it first displayed a regional character owing to the heavy original concentration of expellees and refugees in certain Länder. The success thus far achieved in integrating the refugees seriously threatens the future of the GB-BHE, even though nonparty associations of expellees continue to flourish, hold meetings and issue publications.

There are also several regional or state parties, some of which have long histories but whose present existence has become precarious. Thus there is the German Party (DP), chiefly in Lower Saxony; the Bavarian Party (BP) in Bavaria; and the Center Party (ZP), mainly in North Rhine–Westphalia. In federal politics, the German Party has been an appendage of the CDU; and in July 1960, nine of its fifteen Bundestag members announced that they were joining the CDU.[16] While such parties may disappear at Bonn, they may still have a certain role in state politics.

The Weimar Republic perished in the warfare of the parties of the extreme Right and Left. Article 21 of the West German Constitution, in providing for the banning of these parties, encourages the trend toward the two big parties of the Middle. In 1952, the Federal Constitutional Court declared unconstitutional the (neo-Nazi) *Sozialistische Reichspartei* (SRP) which had developed considerable strength in Lower Saxony.[17] The (neo-Nazi) *Deutsche Reichspartei* (DRP) has not yet been prohibited by the Court although the party has been under heavy attack following the anti-Semitic outrages which occurred in the winter of 1959-1960.[18] In 1956, the nationwide German Communist Party (KPD) was outlawed by the Federal Constitutional Court.[19] In spite of this and in spite of the vigilance of the authorities, a vigorous Communist "underground" exists in West Germany.[20]

As in the United States, the same party system operates at both federal and state levels, with federal and state politics reacting upon each other. The Landtag elections occur at regular intervals within the four-year term of the Bundestag and are often interpreted as indirect federal elections.[21] This is because they can affect the control of state votes in the Bundesrat (the upper house of the Federal Parliament) which, as will subsequently be indicated, has important legislative and administrative powers.[22] The downfall of the Arnold Cabinet in North Rhine–Westphalia (1956) and of the Hoegner Cabinet in Bavaria (1957) illustrate the interaction of federal and state politics. Each of these cases resulted in a change in the party control of the state delegation in the Bundesrat.

On the other hand, state politics cannot be described solely as the reflection of federal politics.[23] The holding of Bundestag and Landtag elections at different times facilitates emphasis on state personalities and issues and encourages more discriminating voting.[24] For example, the great Adenauer victory in the September 1957 Bundestag election was not duplicated in the Hamburg state legislature election of November 1957 when Max Brauer and the SPD were decisively returned to power.[25]

In both the United States and West Germany, federal elections generally arouse greater interest and participation than do state elections. In the Bundestag elections of 1949, 1953 and 1957, the percentages of registered citizens voting were respectively 78.5, 86.0, and 88.2 percent. In Landtag elections, the range is usually from 70 to 80 percent, but higher figures are sometimes reached as in 1955 at the Bremen election (84 percent) .[26] The discrepancy in popular support between the two sets of polls has not affected all parties equally; it is said to be especially characteristic of CDU-CSU women voters whose interest tends to be greater in federal elections.[27]

Although the three largest parties (CDU, SPD, FDP) are national in scope,[28] they are not highly centralized because of the checks inherent in a federal form of government.[29]

The principal units of these parties are generally Land organizations or organizations in areas which were formerly Länder or provinces. The SPD has twenty-one districts (*Bezirke*). The CDU has sixteen Land organizations (*Landes-verbände*), and is in theory more federal in structure than the SPD. While the SPD historically has been more centralized than its rivals, the Social Democrats of Bavaria, Bremen, and Hamburg have not always seen eye to eye with the national leadership. Moreover, since the CDU appeals to "all sorts and conditions of men," the SPD is also moving to broaden its base, a fact which operates against doctrinaire control from headquarters. The SPD platform was changed in November 1959 so as to abandon much of the party's traditional Marxism; there is likewise a "new look" in Social Democratic foreign policy.[30]

"Broadening the base," however, is not necessarily synonymous with more democratization in practice. Even in the SPD, which has long stressed party democracy, criticism has been expressed of the party "apparatus" or machine. West German parties are still far from being fully democratic in their organization, operation, and financing. The ideal expressed in Article 21-1 of the Federal Constitution is praiseworthy; but legislation to implement the article has thus far proven impossible to enact,[31] chiefly because of questions relating to party finance.[32] Otto Kirkheimer has pointed out that, since only about 3 percent of the voters are enrolled as members of political parties, the average citizen enters the political arena indirectly through affiliation with interest groups. He thus has "only an election-day choice between party machines whose conduct he neither influences nor seeks to influence."[33]

Election Legislation

The West German road toward a two-party system has been in part constructed by election laws.[34] These usually discourage small "splinter" parties by various requirements, the most common being the 5 percent rule. Thus in Rhineland-Palatinate, a party or political group which does not poll 5 percent of the valid ballots cast is disregarded in the allocation of legislative seats. In North Rhine–Westphalia, as will be explained below, the 5 percent rule is likewise used but a party may still qualify if it is able to elect at least one candidate in a single-member district.

Notwithstanding the trend to the two-party system, West German election legislation is still far from the customary pattern in the United States. American state legislatures are ordinarily chosen by plurality vote from single-member districts, each voter voting for one candidate. This is what the Germans call *"Mehrheitswahl."* It contrasts with proportional representation (*Verhältniswahl*) under which parties are represented in legislative bodies in proportion to the votes which they receive. The Germans have long debated the merits and disadvantages of these two forms of election. The present laws governing Landtag elections generally attempt to combine the two, although in Bremen and Rhineland-Palatinate strict proportional representation is followed.

Thus in Land Bremen, there are two constituencies, the city of Bremen (which chooses eighty members of the state legislature) and the city of Bremerhaven (which chooses twenty members). The electors vote only for party lists of candidates; the seats are assigned to the parties by the d'Hondt quota plan in proportion to the ballots received by the party tickets, disregarding such parties as fail to reach the 5 percent minimum.

However, most of the Länder have mixed systems which may deviate considerably from mathematical proportional representation. In North Rhine–Westphalia, for example, there are 150 single-member districts in which a mere plurality is enough to elect. There are also fifty seats filled from a Land reserve list. The total votes received by all the parties in the 150 constituencies are tabulated, after which the votes of parties failing to meet one or the other of the minimum requirements are disregarded. The net totals are then used in computing how many of the two hundred seats each of the qualifying parties is entitled to have. A party which has secured more than this total quota through elections in the 150 constituencies keeps all the seats won there. The fifty seats on the Land list are then apportioned among the other parties which have received less than their quotas.

Whether chosen by proportional representation or by a mixed system, the Landtag normally consists of representatives of three or more parties, no one of which has a majority. Hence a coalition cabinet is necessary. Single parties have occasionally won more than half of the legislative seats, as happened in Bavaria and North Rhine–Westphalia in 1958, and in Bremen and Rhineland-Palatinate in 1959. Such a situation sometimes has produced a one-party cabinet, of which there have been six thus far. Three of these were SPD: Hamburg (1950-1953); Hesse (1951-1954); and Schleswig-Holstein (1947-1950). There have been three CDU or CSU cabinets: South Baden (CDU, 1949-1952, before the formation of Baden-Württemberg); Bavaria (CSU, 1947-1950); and North Rhine–Westphalia (CDU, 1958–).[35] On the other hand, in the Hamburg election of November 1957 and in the Bremen election of October 1959, the SPD had an absolute majority both of the popular vote and of the seats in the legislature. Nevertheless, the SPD chose to form coalition cabinets with the FDP.[36]

The coalition cabinet may contain members from all the parties represented in the Landtag. This was the case in Baden-Württemberg from October 1953 until after the Landtag election of May 1960. It was made necessary by the secessionist threat of the *Altbadener*. The coalition fell apart when the 1960 election exposed the weakness of those who wanted to restore the former state of Baden.

The coalition may omit some of the minor parties but include the CDU and SPD, as did the cabinet of Lower Saxony formed in November 1957 by Minister-President Heinrich Hellwege (DP).[37] Another example was the CDU-SPD-FDP cabinet in Bremen (1951-1959). A CDU-SPD combination is often called a "great coalition" to distinguish it from the more typical "little coalition" built around either the CDU or SPD. In any event, the formation of a coalition regime means protracted negotiations between the parties concerning the allocation of cabinet posts and the policies to be followed.

Initiative and Referendum

In West Germany, representative or "indirect democracy" is the dominant pattern. A Landtag election is sometimes informally called a "referendum." The present discussion is not concerned with that meaning of the word but with the popular initiative and referendum ("*Volksbegehren*" and "*Volksentscheid*") such as are formally authorized in a number of American states. Although the constitutions of Baden-Württemberg, Bavaria, Bremen, Hesse, North Rhine–Westphalia, Rhineland-Palatinate, and the Saar contain various provisions on the subject, these devices of "direct democracy" have been little used in the Bundesrepublik. As previously noted, there have been referenda on five state constitutions and on one constitutional amendment. However, in general, direct democracy is less stressed than in the Weimar Republic; it is chiefly exemplified by the "town meeting" (*Gemeindeversammlung*) in the smallest municipalities of several states. Thus in Hesse, for *Gemeinden* of not more than one hundred inhabitants, the *Gemeindeversammlung* is used in place of the elected council.[38]

From the earlier analysis, it will be recalled that the

Grundgesetz (Articles 29, 118) authorized referenda on certain territorial rearrangements, but that hitherto the only popular voting was on the formation of the Southwest State. (The 1955 referendum on the status of the Saar was held before the Saar became a German Land.) [39] There are also cases where similar referenda are mandatory in local government. For example, in Bavaria, *Gemeinden* cannot be abolished or annexed in whole or in part without a favorable vote of the citizens concerned.[40]

In contrast to the official initiative and referendum, there has been increasing use of public opinion polls.[41] In the decade following World War II, there were numerous polls of the German population by the Office of Military Government for Germany (US) and by its successor, the Office of the U.S. High Commissioner for Germany. During the same period, private German agencies also developed, notably the Institute for Market and Opinion Research (EMNID) in Bielefeld, the *Institut für Demoskopie* in Allensbach, and the *Deutsches Institut für Volksumfragen* (DIVO) in Frankfurt. These surveys have sampled opinion on a wide range of topics. They have included questions on state government, a subject on which German (as well as American) citizens have not particularly distinguished themselves by their knowledge.[42]

May a state or local government conduct an advisory popular referendum on a federal matter such as foreign policy or defense? This issue has been raised several times since the Bundesrepublik was launched in 1949. That was also the year when the Council of Europe came into existence and when the European Union of Federalists began to urge that the peoples of Europe be given an opportunity to vote on continental federation. With this stimulus, in July 1950 the voters of the cities of Castrop-Rauxel (North Rhine–Westphalia) and Breisach (South Baden) voted an overwhelming "Yes" on the question, "Do you favor the abolition of political and economic frontiers in Europe and the unification of all European peoples in a European federal state?" The referenda were sponsored by the German branch of the European Union of Federalists but were actively promoted by the two local governments concerned. They were opposed by the Communists.[43]

Shortly before these referenda, the Korean War broke out. It quickly caused the Western Allies to reverse their policy on German disarmament and to urge the Federal Republic's participation in the defense of Europe against Communist aggression. This sudden switch produced a heated controversy among the West Germans, some of whom called for a popular referendum. For example, a Communist organization (*Hauptausschuss für Volksbefragung*) proposed a referendum on the question, "Are you against the remilitarization of Germany and for a peace treaty with Germany in 1951?" However, on April 26, 1951, the Federal Minister of the Interior forbade the referendum. While noting that he did not object to unofficial polls as such, he held that the sponsoring organization was an unconstitutional association under Article 9 of the *Grundgesetz*.[44]

Another great debate centered on the vote of the Bundestag (March 25, 1958) which authorized the equipment of the military forces (*Bundeswehr*) with tactical nuclear weapons. Beaten on the main issue, the SPD members of the Bundestag sought to force a nationwide referendum on atomic rearmament.[45] This too was defeated, the Bundestag majority affirming that the West German Constitution made no provision for any kind of popular referendum except on territorial changes under Articles 29 and 118.

Bremen and Hamburg thereupon passed legislation calling for their own state referenda.[46] The Federal Cabinet and the Bundestag majority challenged the two laws and appealed to the Federal Constitutional Court which, on July 30, 1958, held them unconstitutional.[47] According to the Court, these Land enactments attempted to provide for citizen participation in a matter under exclusive federal jurisdiction. Moreover, since the structure of the Bundesrat precludes direct instructions from the people of a state to their representatives in that body, referenda designed to accomplish the purpose are inadmissible.

Land Hesse was also haled before the Court. No statewide vote was planned there, but the state did not object to three Hessian cities holding referenda. The court found that Hesse had violated its obligation of loyalty to the constitutionally established pattern of federal-state relationships by not annulling the resolutions of the three cities which had authorized referenda.[48]

STATE CABINETS AND LEGISLATURES

The United States Constitution guarantees to every state "a republican form of government" and prohibits the denial to American citizens of the right to vote because of race, color, or sex. The West German Constitution is more explicit. Article 28 declares that "the constitutional order in the Länder must conform to the principles of republican, democratic and social government based on the rule of law, within the meaning of the *Grundgesetz.*" Moreover, the states and their counties and municipalities must have popularly elected legislatures chosen by "universal, direct, free, equal and secret elections."[49] State cabinets and legislatures, therefore, must be established in accordance with these requirements.[50]

Cabinet Responsibility to the Legislature

Whatever latitude the *Grundgesetz* may give in state executive-legislative relationships, the Land constitutions prescribe the parliamentary form of government.[51] The Landtag elects the minister-president who is chief of the cabinet (*Landesregierung*) and who also usually performs various formal duties as head of the state. The other cabinet members are named by the minister-president and are usually individually or collectively approved by the legislature.[52]

In size, the cabinet ranges from six in Rhineland-Palatinate to fifteen in Bavaria where state secretaries are also included. With the exception of the minister-president, each person heads a ministry, or two or three portfolios may be combined under one man. The list of positions always includes the four "classical" ministries—interior, finance, justice and *Kultus* (education, religion, and cultural affairs) —to which are usually added economics, labor, and agriculture. There have been attempts to reduce the number of cabinet posts. This, however, is difficult politically where it affects the allocation of jobs among the parties in the governing coalition.

While stipulating that the *Landesregierung* shall be responsible to the legislature, state constitutions take note of the unhappy experiences of the Weimar period and endeavor to lessen cabinet instability. There are certain requirements for the vote of no confidence, such as appropriate advance notice of the motion, and adoption of that motion by a majority of the whole membership of the Landtag. Like the Federal Republic (Article 67), six states have the so-called "positive" or "constructive" vote of no confidence (*konstruktives Misstrauensvotum*). This means that, in denying confidence to the minister-president and his cabinet, the legislature must at the same time elect his successor.

In the other four Länder, the procedure is somewhat different. Thus in Hesse, Rhineland-Palatinate and the Saar, a cabinet overturn through a no-confidence motion must be followed within a specified time by legislative approval of a new cabinet or the Landtag is automatically dissolved. In Bavaria (Article 44), the minister-president "must resign if the political situation makes cooperation between him and the Landtag impossible." If the legislature fails to name a successor within four weeks of the resignation, it must be dissolved.

Thus far there has been only one case where the *konstruktives Misstrauensvotum* has been successfully used. This involved the CDU-FDP-ZP cabinet in North Rhine–Westphalia headed by the late Karl Arnold. The FDP of that state revolted against the Adenauer regime and policies at Bonn and joined with the SPD in a no-confidence motion. On February 20, 1956, the motion was carried by a vote of 102 to 96; it named Fritz Steinhoff (SPD) as minister-president who formed a new coalition cabinet (SPD-FDP-ZP) .[53]

But in general, cabinets or ministers are more apt to resign without formal legislative action, particularly if the coalition breaks up. On October 8, 1957, after the withdrawal of the Bavarian Party and Refugee Party members from the cabinet, Minister-President Wilhelm Hoegner (SPD) of Bavaria quit.[54] The short-lived Bartram cabinet in Schleswig-Holstein (1950-1951) aroused great objections because of former connections with the National Socialists. After nine months, Minister-President Walter Bartram gave up his office.[55]

In May 1955, Franz Leonhard Schlueter, who belonged to the right wing of the FDP and had neo-Nazi sympathies, was named Minister of Education in Lower Saxony. As soon as the appointment became known, the rector and senate of Göttingen University resigned in protest and the students went on a strike. The pressure of hostile public opinion was such that Schlueter soon resigned.[56] In December 1957, Hans Adolf Asbach, a minister in the Schleswig-Holstein cabinet, was dismissed by Minister-President Kai-Uwe von Hassel for "incompetence." Asbach was orginally appointed by Bartram and, in spite of criticisms, was kept on in succeeding cabinets because his party (the Refugee Party) was in the coalition.[57]

Such examples are rare. Although coalition governments are often unstable, state cabinet personnel displays considerable permanence. There are many veteran Land ministers, some of whom have been continuously in office for more than ten years. Among them are Wilhelm Kaisen (SPD), the head of the Bremen cabinet since 1945, and Peter Altmeier (CDU), Minister-President of Rhineland-Palatinate since 1947. Hinrich Kopf (SPD) of Lower Saxony and Hans Ehard (CSU) of Bavaria are old-time ministers-president, dating from 1946 and in office in 1960, although their service as cabinet chiefs has not been continuous. These illustrations confirm the popular saying, "To become a minister is very hard; to remain a minister is not so very hard."[58]

The State Legislature: Membership[59]

The state legislature is everywhere unicameral except in Bavaria where there is an advisory upper house (*Senat*). The Bavarian Senate, according to Article 34 of the Constitution, represents "the social, economic, cultural and municipal groups of the Land." It has sixty members elected by the constituent groups. The term of office is six years, one-third of the membership retiring every two years. Directly or through the cabinet, the Senate may introduce bills into the Landtag; may prepare opinions on important cabinet bills and may file objections to bills passed by the Landtag. The latter "decides if it wishes to take account of the objections" (Article 41). Experience has shown that the views of the Senate are not without influence on the Landtag.[60]

The Landtag is elected by universal adult suffrage as the organ of representative democracy. The minimum voting age is uniformly twenty-one years, the same as for the Bundestag and for county and municipal councils. The Landtag usually has 100 or more members (*Abgeordnete*) and in this respect is comparable with the lower house of an American state legislature. The Landtag of Bavaria with 204 members is the largest; at the opposite end of the scale, the Saar has 50 members. Although men and women are equally eligible for election, women in 1954 numbered only 7.4 percent of the total number of *Abgeordneten*.[61] Even so, the record is better than in American state legislatures which in 1959 had 347 women out of nearly 8,000 members.[62]

What are the occupations of the representatives? Although studies have been made of the professional backgrounds of Bundestag members,[63] less information of this character has been compiled for the state legislatures. There are similarities in the composition of the Bundestag and the Landtag, in part because so many Bundestag members are persons with experience in state legislatures.[64]

At both the federal and state level, election by proportional representation of at least a part of the membership facilitates the representation of organized groups. "P.R." permits the construction of "balanced tickets" made up of candidates from the various interests to which the parties appeal for votes and financial support. Kirchheimer has noted that "present-day legislatures show a built-in structure of interest representation within the parties' parliamentary groups."[65] The labor union or the industrial association has its full-time officers as members of the representative body. The political party, too, does not forget to nominate its own functionaries. Members of local government councils may also be elected to the state legislature.

Public officials constitute another important element in the Landtag. Unlike Britain and the United States, civil servants are permitted to be deputies without, however, relinquishing their government positions and salaries. Although the British and American occupation authorities made strenuous efforts to change this practice, they were, on the whole, defeated by German resistance.[66] To be sure, some German legislation was passed such as the North Rhine–Westphalia election law of 1950 which required state officials to resign before becoming candidates for the Landtag.[67] On the other hand, in the Bavarian Landtag (1957), more than 80 of the 204 members received fixed salaries as officials of state or local government.[68]

This last statement, however, requires further explanation. One must distinguish between the career official and the politically appointed official; there is more party patronage now than in the days of the Weimar Republic.[69] A *Landrat* (county director) or a *Bürgermeister* must usually be regarded as much more a political than a career official. Deputies who are in the latter category are few.[70]

Dual officeholding raises the problem of conflict of interests. How shall the *Abgeordnete,* who is also a civil servant, act in the Landtag when his official interests are involved? Or, for that matter, how shall the representative of an organized labor or industrial group vote under such circumstances?[71] Although the basic laws on municipal government (*Gemeindeordnungen*) generally contain conflict-of-interest provisions, the only state constitution which has a similar regulation is Bremen (Article 84).

The question is not merely one of legal prohibitions; it also involves the deputy's compensation. According to traditional theory, his post is *ehrenamtlich;* in other words, it is "honorary," part-time, and lay rather than full-time and professional. The Landtag representative thus receives, not a salary, but an *Entschädigung* which is supposed to compensate him for his expenses and loss of time.[72] The Constitutions of Baden-Württemberg (Article 40) and Lower Saxony (Article 17) go further and assert that the *Entschädigung* ought to secure the independence of the deputy. However, in practice he must frequently depend upon an "outside salary" if he is to continue to serve. A strong case can be made for more adequate legislative pay as a means of increasing the deputy's independence and of attracting better personnel.[73] To accomplish this, it is desirable, although politically difficult, to reduce somewhat the size of the legislature.

The members of the state legislatures are elected for four-year terms which, however, may be cut short by dissolution. Except in Baden-Württemberg and Bremen, the Landtag has power to vote its own dissolution; moreover, failure to elect a minister-president within a stated time brings automatic dissolution. In Baden-Württemberg and Bavaria, a recall election may be held if the prescribed number of voters petition for it; thus far, this has never happened. The Bavarian requirement (Article 18) of one million signatures on a recall petition is a formidable obstacle. Baden-Württemberg specifies 200,000 signatures. In the old state of Württemberg-Baden (now a part of Baden-Württemberg), a group of citizens in 1950 attempted to secure a popular vote on the dissolution of the Landtag. The endeavor failed because the sponsors secured only 14,202 signatures instead of the 100,000 then required.[74]

What is obviously not granted is the power of the minister-president or cabinet to dissolve the Landtag; the lesson from the Reichstag dissolutions of 1930-1933 has been well learned. In only two states, Schleswig-Holstein and North Rhine–Westphalia, is there anything approaching such authority and it is carefully safeguarded. In Schleswig-Holstein (Article 31), if the minister-president requests but fails to secure a vote of confidence from the Landtag, he may within ten days dissolve that body—unless the Landtag has meanwhile elected another minister-president. In North Rhine–Westphalia (Article 68), if the legislature rejects a cabinet bill, the cabinet may submit it to popular vote. If the electorate passes the bill, the cabinet may dissolve the Landtag; but if the bill is rejected at the polls, the cabinet must resign.

The State Legislature at Work

State legislative activity is small in volume and scope compared to what it was before the establishment of the Federal Republic in 1949. Nevertheless, an examination of the official gazettes,[75] published by the Länder, shows that, in addition to the voting of the budget, some statutes are enacted at each session.[76] Certain of these, such as laws on education, police, and local government, may be of permanent importance;[77] others are of a more transitory character.

How well equipped is the Landtag to perform its legislative functions? American state lawmakers, who are accustomed to legislative reference and bill-drafting services, will find that these are practically non-existent in the Federal Republic. Lower Saxony (1956) was the first state to appropriate funds to set up a *Gesetzgebungs- und Beratungsdienst* for the use of the deputies.[78] On the other hand, it must be remembered that the West German Länder have a parliamentary form of government with a strong tradition of executive leadership. It is, therefore, not surprising that most bills are formulated and introduced by the cabinet with the assistance of the ministerial bureaucracy.

In spite of this, the Landtag is not a mere rubber stamp; legislative consideration sometimes results in significant amendments to measures. Executive leadership is even more apparent with respect to budgetary questions, although the finance or budget committee of the Landtag and the audit court (*Rechnungshof*) [79] do provide some check on irregularities and uneconomical administration. Even so, legislative control of expenditures, whether in West Germany or in the United States, leaves much to be desired.[80]

As in the Bundestag, the formal organization and proceedings[81] of the Landtag are governed by constitutional provisions and by its own rules (*Geschäftsordnung*). With some modifications, the rules are much like those which prevailed in the Weimar Republic and earlier. They will not be discussed here. There are, however, two subjects which require further comment, namely, the party groups (*Fraktionen*) and the committees of the legislature.[82]

As was the case before the Hitler regime, the deputies are organized into party groups known as *Fraktionen*. These are highly significant committees which are to be distinguished from the duly constituted regular and special committees of the Landtag. In the legislative chamber, the members are seated according to *Fraktionen,* the more radical parties being on the Landtag president's left and the more conservative on his right. Thus the seating arrangement is usually the "Left-Center-Right" pattern customary in many other countries of Western Europe.

To be recognized as a *Fraktion,* a party group must have elected a minimum number of representatives, generally not less than five. The *Abgeordneten* of parties which fail to reach the minimum may combine with each other or with independents to qualify as a *Fraktion.* As an alternative, they may be received into other *Fraktionen* as "guests."

The *Fraktion* meets in secret caucus to determine the party's position on pending issues. Its deliberations may be influenced by the party organization outside the Landtag. Indeed, that organization is likely to be able to speak through *Fraktion* members who are themselves party officials. On the other hand, the nature of the legislature's business is such that real discussion may be required to reach agreement within the group. Although "free voting" on the floor of the chamber may be permitted in specific instances, group decisions, once taken, are normally binding on all members (*Fraktionszwang*) and can be enforced by exclusion from the *Fraktion* or from subsequent candidature on the party ticket.

There has been much German criticism of *Fraktionszwang* as restricting the deputy's independence which is proclaimed in most of the state constitutions. For example, the Schleswig-Holstein *Landessatzung* (Article 9) states that the *Abgeordneten* are:

> representatives of the people. In the exercise of their office, they are subject only to their conscience and are not bound by orders and instructions.

It is hard to see how this traditional principle, if strictly applied, can be reconciled with stable parliamentary government operating through parties. The "independence" of the representative is perhaps better illustrated by the debates and compromises reached within the *Fraktion* meeting.[83]

Turning next to the regular or standing committees, one of the most important is the Council of Elders (*Ältestenrat*). It is composed of the president and vice presidents of the Landtag and a small number of deputies named by the *Fraktionen* in proportion to their party strength. The *Fraktion* leaders are generally members of the Council of Elders. The *Ältestenrat* controls the calendar of the house. It is the agency for reaching or attempting to reach intergroup decisions, especially those involving political dynamite. It may also be entrusted with the assignment of committee chairmanships, these being allocated according to party strength in the coalition.

As in most legislatures, the bulk of work in lawmaking and in supervising administration falls to the standing committees. Nominally elected by the Landtag, they are in fact chosen by the *Fraktionen* so as to insure proportional representation of the parties. *Fraktion* (and hence party) influence is thus exercised through its deputies on the committees, but with less opportunity for *Fraktionszwang* than in the plenary sessions of the Landtag. The *Fraktion* also endeavors to distribute its members so that those having knowledge of a particular ministry or function will be on the committee having jurisdiction thereof. In West Germany as in the United States, long committee service may develop expertness. This is a valuable counterweight against the pressure of ministers who, with the support of the ministerial bureaucracy, pilot the cabinet bills constituting most of the committee agenda.

The number of standing committees ranges from 11 in Hesse and Rhineland-Palatinate to 27 in North Rhine–Westphalia, a high figure likely to increase the referring of bills after the first reading to more than one committee. Fewer committees with appropriate subcommittees would be preferable; the latter are in any event likely to be used on important measures. Except in Bavaria, committee sessions are not open to the public. This undemocratic practice may justifiably be criticized, especially since decisions hammered out in committee are not lightly overturned by the Landtag on the subsequent reading or readings.[84]

In addition to the standing committees, special investigating committees may also be created. They are, however, less common than in American state legislatures and are usually precipitated by irregularities of one kind or another. The Auerbach case in Bavaria (1951-1953) involved the state restitution office (*Landesentschädigungsamt*).[85] Another Bavarian example (1955-1960) had to do with gambling casino (*Spielbank*) concessions.[86] In 1955, the Landtag of Lower Saxony appointed a special committee to look into the Schlueter case, mentioned earlier in this study.[87]

The present chapter has examined certain main features of state government. Attention will next be turned to the important subject of federal-state relations.

3 BUND AND LAENDER

The previous discussion has examined the Länder with respect to such matters as area, population, resources, political parties, and constitutional and governmental structure. These are important for judging the effectiveness of the constituent units in a federal system, but they are not the only factors to be considered. A further question must be asked. Do the states have any significant authority which they can exercise at their own discretion, or are they merely ministerial agents of the Bund?

West German federalism came into existence after much dispute and disagreement among the Western Allies and the Germans.[1] It represented a conscious and, on the whole, successful effort to overcome the shortcomings of the Weimar Republic. After over a decade of experience, the undertaking has achieved a certain stability; in spite of continuing German criticism,[2] it is a "going federal concern." This achievement is in no small part due to the Bundesrat, the upper house of the Federal Parliament.[3]

THE BUNDESRAT

The lower house of Parliament (Bundestag) is far from possessing the powers of a unicameral legislature; the vital role of the Bundesrat and of its committees must also be stressed.[4] According to the *Grundgesetz* (Article 50), "the Länder, through the Bundesrat, cooperate in the legislation and administration of the Bund." Armed with the right of judicial review, the United States Supreme Court is often described as the "balance wheel" of the American federal system. While the Federal Constitutional Court in West Germany has similar authority and has used it effectively,[5] its action is intermittent rather than continuous. The Bundesrat, on the other hand, is a continuously operating "balance wheel." In the language of intergovernmental relations, it is the major focus of federal-state cooperation—and also of conflict.[6] As the organ and voice of the Länder, it links the Bund and the states together in a more intimate fashion than in American federalism.

In the Bundesrat, each state has as many members as it has votes. The number varies somewhat according to population, but it is never less than three nor more than five per state. The total membership now stands at forty-one, not counting the four nonvoting representatives from West Berlin. The votes of a given Land are cast as a bloc under instructions from the state cabinet which chooses ministers from its own ranks to sit in the Bundesrat. The minister-president is usually one of those named.

On the thirteen standing committees of the Bundesrat where the bulk of the work is done, the ministers are generally represented by career ministerial officials as their deputies, a fact which contributes to the high professional competence of the upper house. For this reason, the Bundesrat has been called the "Parliament of the learned priests," and has been contrasted with the Bundestag, the "Parliament of the lay brothers."[7]

The Federal Cabinet is closely associated with the Bundesrat and includes the Ministry for Bundesrat Affairs,[8] which is at present headed by a confirmed federalist, Dr. Hans-Joachim von Merkatz (formerly DP and now CDU).[9] Cabinet members may be present at the sessions of the Bundesrat and of its committees; they may speak and be questioned but are without voting rights. Moreover, informal as well as formal contacts are numerous.

According to the letter of the Federal Constitution, the legislative authority of the Bundesrat is not equal to that of the Bundestag. However, as recent studies have shown,[10] such authority has developed greatly in practice. The Bundesrat has become a more powerful second chamber than the constitutional fathers had envisaged. Its method of selection insures that it will reflect the results of recurring Landtag elections and thus mirror state or regional opinion.

In legislation, the Bundesrat is very influential. If the Bundesrat does not agree with a measure passed by the Bundestag, it may demand consideration of it by a joint conference committee (*Vermittlungsausschuss*) of the two houses. If disagreement still persists, the Bundesrat has either an absolute or a suspensory veto. The veto is absolute in the case of constitutional amendments and of certain types of bills affecting the Länder; these must have specific Bundesrat consent (*Zustimmung*). (There is also a wide range of federal administrative ordinances which require Bundesrat approval.) For other proposed statutes not needing consent, the veto (*Einspruch*) of the Bundesrat may be overridden by the Bundestag. The veto necessary for the Bundestag to set aside a veto depends upon the size of the majority supporting the veto in the Bundesrat.

FEDERAL-STATE RELATIONS IN LEGISLATION

The distribution of federal and state powers in the American Constitution is familiar. The Tenth Amendment to that document declares: "The powers not delegated to the United States by the Constitution, nor prohibited by it to the States, are reserved to the States respectively, or to the people." This may be compared with Articles 30 and 70 of the *Grundgesetz* which read:

The exercise of governmental (*staatlichen*) powers and the performance of governmental functions is the concern of the Länder insofar as this Constitution does not otherwise prescribe or permit.

The Länder have the right of legislation insofar as this Constitution does not grant legislative powers to the Bund. . . .

In Articles 71 through 75, three lists of legislative subjects are enumerated: those exclusively reserved to the Bund, eleven in number; twenty-three concurrent fields; and five categories in which the Bund may establish general principles or standards (*Rahmenvorschriften*). Among the first group are foreign affairs; defense; postal and telecommunications; and federal railways and air traffic. On such matters, the states may legislate only if they are expressly authorized to do so by federal law. Under *Rahmenvorschriften*, to mention several examples, one finds state and local government civil service; press and motion pictures; and registration of persons (*Melde- und Ausweisewesen*).

As for the concurrent fields, Article 72 states that the Länder may enact laws "so long as and insofar as the Bund has made no use of its legislative rights." Moreover, with respect to these twenty-three categories, the Bund has almost a *carte blanche*. It may legislate where:

1. A matter cannot be effectively regulated through the legislation of the individual Länder, or

2. The regulation of a matter by Land law can prejudice the interests of other Länder or of the whole (nation), or

3. The maintenance of legal and economic unity requires it, especially the maintenance of uniformity of living conditions extending beyond the territory of a Land.

Article 72 recognizes what existed in German federalism before 1933, namely, a high degree of federal legislative uniformity, much greater than is found in the United States.

Acting under its constitutional mandate, the Federal Parliament has already enacted an impressive number of statutes. The zonal fragmentation of lawmaking, which characterized the military government period (1945-1949), has been largely overcome in West Germany. Thus in the administration of justice, the law has once again been unified.[11] The same is true in most economic spheres, a notable example being the replacement of the federally organized *Bank deutscher Länder* (1948) by the centralized *Deutsche Bundesbank* (1957).[12] Unlike the previous banking system,[13] the role of the states has become minimal; they are even required to use the Bank as the depository for their funds.[14]

Nevertheless, there are several important subjects, such as local government, police, and education and cultural affairs, which are not mentioned in the concurrent list set forth in Article 74. In these fields, as will be shown later, the states initiate and enact the laws; the federal interest is either peripheral or nonexistent. Nor does this exhaust the legislative functions of the Länder. Through the Bundesrat and through less formal federal-state discussions, they actively participate in all federal lawmaking. For example, a reform of the Corporation Act of 1937 is now under way. The first draft of a bill, written by the bureaucracy of the Federal Ministry of Economics, was discussed in 1959 by a special working party set up by the state ministers of economics. The working party submitted fifty-one pages of comments and suggestions.[15] This kind of consultation is a regular occurrence in the legislative process at Bonn.

FEDERAL-STATE RELATIONS IN ADMINISTRATION

In the United States, the traditional pattern has been that federal functions are directly administered by federal agencies. There are, of course, some exceptions to this rule. From the beginning, the states have been used as agents for the conduct of federal elections.[16] Moreover, the rise of a vast system of conditional federal grants-in-aid has, in effect, enlarged the agency role of the states. But on the whole, direct federal administration still prevails in America.

The situation is different in the Bundesrepublik. According to the Constitution (Article 83), "the states execute federal laws as matters of their own concern insofar as this *Grundgesetz* does not otherwise prescribe or permit." This principle has a long history. State administration of federal laws characterized the German Empire founded by Bismarck. The same was true of the Weimar Republic, in spite of the creation of much direct federal administrative machinery, a development which the Bonn Constitution endeavors to restrain in favor of the older principle. In practice, this has resulted in a system where "the Federal Government does most of the legislating while the Länder do most of the administering,"[17] a kind of division of power between federal legislation and state administration.

Eschenburg distinguishes seven types of federal and state administration as follows:[18]

1. Federal administration (*bundeseigene Verwaltung*) at the federal level (Foreign Office, Federal Statistical Office).

2. Federal administration within the Bund and the states (Federal Post Office).

3. Direct federal public law corporation (Federal Institution for Employment Service and Unemployment Insurance).

4. State administration (*landeseigene Verwaltung*) in the execution of federal laws (jurisdiction of the police in highway traffic regulation).

5. State administration in the execution of state laws (education).

6. State administration as delegated administration (*Auftragsverwaltung*) of the Bund (federal superhighways).

7. Public law corporations and institutions of the Länder, which may be either self-governing bodies (municipalities, chambers of commerce); or delegated state administration (registrar's office or *Standesamt*) in municipalities.

For some functions in which the Bund has exclusive legislative authority (the federal railways and the postal service), there is direct federal administration without state participation, as provided in Articles 86 and 87 of the *Grundgesetz*. For other activities (federal canals and highways), there may be a mixture of direct and delegated federal administration, as seen in Articles 89 and 90. To the extent that state agencies are used in delegated federal administration, they are subject to federal orders (*Weisungen*).

So far as the concurrent powers are concerned, the basic assumption is that the states execute federal laws as *landeseigene Verwaltung*. This involves less supervision from Bonn than does federal *Auftragsverwaltung*. The consequence is that the federal ministries often consist only of small central staffs, since their field administration is handled by the Länder.

The extent of state administration of federal law is shown by the following statistics.[19] In 1955, there were in West Germany 2,417,833 persons employed in direct, full-time government service. The Bund had 958,421, but 813,832 of these were railway and postal employees. By 1959, the total for the Bund had risen to about 1,000,000 exclusive of the armed forces and the Ministry of Defense.[20] In 1955, the Länder had 671,463 on their payrolls;[21] and the local governments, 473,272. If railway, postal and military personnel are disregarded, it is apparent that, in the civil service, the Bund ranks numerically well below the states and the local governments where the main burden of administration rests.

Under the United States and the West German Constitutions, various types of formal and informal intergovernmental cooperation have been developed between the central government and the states.[22] In addition to state administration of the laws of the Bundesrepublik, other examples may be cited.[23]

Americans are familiar with the cooperative arrangements which the Federal Bureau of Investigation has with state and local police authorities. Somewhat similar roles are played in West Germany by the Federal Criminal Police Office (*Bundeskriminalpolizeiamt*) and the Federal Office for the Protection of the Constitution (*Bundesamt für Verfassungsschutz*). The *Grundgesetz* (Article 73-10) gives the Bund exclusive legislative authority over "cooperation of the Bund and Länder in criminal police and in matters of the protection of the Constitution. . . ." The Federal Parliament has passed two laws to implement this provision. These require each Land to establish a state criminal police office and a state office for the protection of the Constitution against subversion.[24] The function of protecting the Constitution without violating the rights of individuals is difficult and controversial; in this area, federal-state cooperation has not always been achieved.[25]

Cooperation may involve economic undertakings[26] such as the famous Volkswagen automobile works in Lower Saxony, an enterprise which until recently was an object of dispute between the Bund and the state of Lower Saxony involving the joint trusteeship between the two.[27] It may be expressed in a federal-state administrative agreement (*Verwaltungsabkommen*) such as that of 1957 on planning (*Raumordnung*).[28] In certain fields, it has resulted in the creation by federal laws of federal and state public law corporations organically tied together.[29] Without endeavoring to cover all functions,[30] housing (a subject of the highest importance in the aftermath of war's destruction) will be selected as a good illustration of federal-state administrative and financial cooperation.

"Cooperative Federalism": Housing

In industrialized nations, the provision of housing affords a striking opportunity for the cooperation of all levels of government with each other and with private enterprise. Here the Bundesrepublik has achieved a remarkable record. By the end of World War II, almost 25 percent of the dwellings in West Germany had been destroyed or so severely damaged as to be uninhabitable. From 1948 through 1958, approximately 4,500,000 housing units were built or restored at a cost of more than 78 billion DM. In 1959, 591,000 additional units were added.[31] Even so, there is still a large shortage.

Although the Länder and their local governments have played a great role in housing during the postwar years, only the Constitutions of Bavaria, Bremen, and Rhineland-Palatinate specifically mention housing. According to the Constitution of Bavaria (Article 106) :

> Every inhabitant of Bavaria is entitled to a suitable dwelling. The furthering of the construction of inexpensive homes for the people is a function of the state and of the municipalities. . . .

The framers of the *Grundgesetz* were careful to include housing among the subjects for concurrent legislation. Article 74-18 lists "Transactions in landed property, law concerning land and agricultural leases, housing, settlements and homesteads." Under this authority, the Bund has enacted important legislation, notably, the First Housing Act of 1950, amended in 1953 and the Second Housing Act of 1956.[32]

The Federal Ministry of Housing (*Wohnungsbau*) was one of the original ministries, being created even before the passage of the First Housing Act. Its main emphasis thus far has been on housing construction and repair. Here, it is the central agency for legislative planning, coordination and financing, with administration carried out at state and local levels. In the Länder, housing is usually placed in the ministry of the interior, since this has most to do with local government.[33]

The dwellings constructed in West Germany fall into three main categories: (1) housing built in the free market without government financial aid and also without rent or housing controls; (2) housing built under the stimulus of tax exemptions; and (3) "social housing" (*sozialer Wohnungsbau*). The first group requires no special comment. In the second, firms or individuals who make interest-free loans from their business revenues for certain types of housing may deduct part of any such loan from their taxable income before computing income and corporation taxes.[34] Similarly, the builders of houses may deduct annually over a period of years a portion of the building cost.[35]

By far the most important category is social housing. This is government-promoted; it aims to keep down the rents or carrying charges so that adequate but inexpensive housing will be within the reach of the broad masses of the population. Government financial aid may take one or several forms, such as outright grants, guarantees of loans, loans at low rates of interest, and annual subsidies toward interest payments.[36] The operating agencies are non-profit housing companies (*gemeinnützige Wohnungsbaugesellschaften*) aided by a variety of special credit institutions.[37] The housing company may be set up in different ways. For example, it may be a cooperative organized by a labor union or a church-related group, or it may be established by a municipal government.

The biggest social housing project thus far launched in West Germany is Neue Vahr in Bremen. When completed in 1961, this "garden city" will accommodate 40,000 people. The funds for Neue Vahr are being raised by the *Bremische Gemeinnützige Wohnungsbaugesellschaft* through its large parent company, the labor union cooperative, *Neue Heimat*. The state of Bremen guarantees the sum required and also provides subsidies to keep interest payments, and hence rents, at low levels.[38]

In each of the years from the beginning of 1953 through 1959, over 500,000 housing units have been built annually in West Germany and West Berlin. Except in 1958, over 300,000 social housing units were added each year. The peak was reached in 1956—559,000 housing units built, of which 423,322 or 75.7 percent were social housing units.[39]

Governmental expenditures for the promotion of housing have been consistently large. In 1954, the Bund contributed 900,000,000 DM; the Länder, 912,200,000 DM; and the local governments, 337,300,000 DM. To these must be added the federally controlled equalization of burdens (*Lastenausgleich*) funds. In 1954, 1,034,900,000 DM from this capital levy went for the housing of refugees and war victims.[40]

The Federal Minister of Housing is responsible for the allocation of federal money among the Länder. In consultation with the chief housing officials of the states, he prepares an annual plan of distribution. Although according to the law, the Federal Minister has the last word, in practice the plan is jointly prepared and approved by the state officials concerned. A similar process takes place between the states and their local governments with respect to available funds. Since there is never enough money for everything needing to be done, there is naturally some controversy between rival claims. But on the whole, housing represents a successful federal-state-local partnership.

FEDERAL-STATE FINANCIAL RELATIONS

In West Germany as in the United States, the problem of federal-state financial relations is of the first importance.[41] Prior to the establishment of the Bundesrepublik in 1949, public finance was the responsibility of the Länder, of zonal or bizonal German organizations, and of the Allied military governments. Since then, by federal constitutional provision and statutory enactment, various functions and revenues have been transferred[42] to the Bund and federal-state financial relations have been defined.

The present analysis is concerned primarily with revenues, especially taxes.[43] West Germany is one of the most heavily taxed nations in Western Europe. The combined federal, state, and local taxes (including social insurance taxes) usually amount to a little over 30 percent of the gross annual national product.[44] This high percentage is not surprising. Postwar governmental costs have been enormous and have involved outlays for housing and other types of physical reconstruction; care of refugees; Jewish restitution payments; payments in connection with the London agreements of 1953 concerning the settlement of the pre-Hitler external and internal debts; and numerous other items. In recent years, defense expenditures have risen rapidly, amounting to over 25 percent of the federal budgets voted for 1958-1959 and 1959-1960.[45]

As in the United States, federal state, and local treasuries are under heavy pressure. Hence there is conflict between the levels of government over the allocation of taxes, with the Bund taking the lion's share. In 1958, the "tax cake" (as the Germans call it) was divided as follows:[46]

	DM	Percentage of Total Taxes
Bund	28,964,900,000	53.8
Equalization of Burdens Levy	2,213,100,000	4.1
Länder (including West Berlin)	14,985,000,000	27.8
Local Governments	7,628,000,000	14.1

Finance is one of the most important subjects treated in the *Grundgesetz*. Articles 105-115 (Chapter X) and Articles 120 and 120a contain provisions relating to the distribution

of revenues between the Bund and the Länder. The framing
of these articles proved exceptionally difficult. There was
agreement that the excessive financial centralization of the
Weimar Republic should be avoided but what were the best
ways to accomplish this end? The members of the Bonn
Constitutional Convention (*Parlamentarischer Rat*) dif-
fered among themselves; and there were even greater differences of opinion between the Germans on the one hand
and the American, British, and French military governors
and their advisers on the other.[47] Consequently, the final
text which emerged was very much a compromise.[48]

In spite of the increase in federal centralization since
1949, the compromise has on the whole endured. The transi-
tion years from the old to the new regime were successfully
passed. After much controversy between the Bund and the
Länder, the original provisions were amended in 1955 and
1956 and brought more nearly into accord with German
thinking.[49]

In Articles 105-108 as now worded, specifications are laid
down concerning the power to enact tax legislation; the
distribution of the tax proceeds among the levels of government; and the collection machinery.[50] The Bund has exclusive legislative authority with respect to indirect taxes
such as customs, excises and turnover taxes (*Umsatzsteuer*),
and to government fiscal monopolies such as alcoholic spirits.
Except for a few levies of local application, it has the power
of concurrent legislation over other taxes. However, in this
case there is an important qualification. Federal statutes
relaxing to taxes, the yields of which go partly or wholly to
the Länder or to the local governments, require the approval
of the Bundesrat, that vigilant guardian of the rights of the
states.

Through the exercise of its concurrent authority, the
Bund may leave much or little to state legislation. Thus
the valuation of property for taxation purposes is uniformly

regulated by federal law. While the income and corporation tax is collected by the states, the rates are fixed by the Bund without room for state variation.

As to the distribution of revenues among the levels of government, Article 106 assigns to the Bund the earnings of government fiscal monopolies and seven categories of taxes. In the fiscal year 1956, the chief sources of federal income were:[51]

	DM
Turnover tax	12,276,100,000
Federal share in income & corporation tax	5,012,600,000
Major excise taxes (tobacco, coffee, sugar)	3,397,100,000
Lastenausgleich levy	2,179,400,000
Customs duties	2,013,700,000
Gasoline and oil taxes	1,510,000,000

Article 106 also enumerates the kinds of taxes, the yield from which goes to the Länder or to the local government. In addition to the states' share in the income and corporation tax (the chief source of their tax income), the list includes property taxes on real estate and business (*Realsteuern*), the inheritance tax, and the motor vehicle tax.

The framers of the Bonn Constitution recognized that there were problems both of "vertical" and of "horizontal" finance equalization (*Finanzausgleich*).[52] The former refers to the division of revenues between the Bund and the Länder in the light of their functions.[53] The latter has to do with financial assistance from the wealthier to the poorer states. With respect to both types of equalization, the first arrangements were provisional; final determination was to be made at a later date. This was accomplished by the constitutional amendments of 1955 and 1956 which have already been mentioned.

Under vertical *Finanzausgleich,* one of the most important questions relates to the distribution of the income and corporation tax yield between the Bund and the Länder. This has been a matter of continuing controversy, with the Federal Minister of Finance asking for a larger share and the states, through the Bundesrat, vetoing or reducing the legislative implementation of his requests. At the outset, the Bund received only 17 percent of the income and corporation tax money. As federal financial responsibilities mounted, the percentage was raised so that in some years it was as much as 38 percent. The constitutional amendment of 1955 stipulated that, from April 1, 1958, the Bund should get 35 percent and the Länder 65 percent; but these ratios could be modified every two years by federal legislation which required Bundesrat approval. Moreover, if federal laws impose additional expenditures on the states or decrease their revenues, the states' percentage of the income and corporation tax receipts is to be increased.[54]

Vertical equalization between the Bund and the Länder does not end with the division of the tax proceeds. It may also include general financial allotments (*allgemeine Finanzzuweisungen*) from the Bund to the states. These amounted to 1,046,300,000 DM in 1954, not counting 130,400,000 DM in *Lastenausgleich* funds,[55] nor 735,500,000 DM in federal loans to the states.[56] The wealthy state of North Rhine–Westphalia received no general allotment. On the other hand, the poorest state, Schleswig-Holstein, got the most money—139,300,000 DM in federal allotments and loans.[57]

More important are the federal statutes on housing, refugees, etc. under which the Bund appropriates money to the states for particular purposes. Thus the Second Housing Act[58] fixed the 1957 federal contribution for social housing at 700,000,000 DM. A further example may be cited: state expenditures for refugees and war victims are reimbursed by the Bund in accordance with a schedule laid down in the law.[59]

Unlike American practice, the financial assistance of the

Bund to the states is not usually in the form of "matching grants"; the Länder are not required to make a contribution from their own revenues as a prerequisite for receiving the aid.[60] In the United States, federal conditional grants have been an important device for getting around the constitutional limitations on the powers of Congress. In West Germany, on the other hand, where the Bund has broad concurrent powers of legislation and where the states administer most federal laws, there is less need for a system of conditional subsidies. However, the matching grant has not been completely unknown; it has been used in the Federal Youth Plan and, under certain conditions, in meeting the cost of access roads connecting with the federal highways.[61]

As previously mentioned, financial equalization between governmental units may be vertical or horizontal or both. The necessity, not only for federal but also for state help to the weaker Länder is shown by the following table.[62]

	1955 Per Capita Income in DM	1954 Per Capita Yield of State and Local Taxes in DM
North Rhine–Westphalia	3,223	347.16
Baden-Württemberg	2,862	320.56
Hesse	2,659	277.66
Bavaria	2,338	227.71
Lower Saxony	2,288	224.22
Rhineland-Palatinate	2,172	221.07
Schleswig-Holstein	1,971	184.79

If the city-states of Hamburg and Bremen were included, the spread would be even greater. In 1955, the per capita income in Hamburg was the highest in West Germany— 4,382 DM or 159 percent of the West German per capita income which was 2,758 DM. The corresponding figures for Bremen in the same year were 3,915 DM or 142 percent. At the bottom of the scale, Schleswig-Holstein had only 71 percent of the national average; while Bavaria, Lower Saxony and Rhineland-Palatinate had 86, 83, and 79 percent respectively. Although previously noted in this study, it should be recalled that Schleswig-Holstein, Lower Saxony and Bavaria received the largest number of refugees in the early postwar years.

Being the financially weakest partner, Schleswig-Holstein has received substantial sums from the Bund and from the wealthier Länder. In the fiscal year 1951-1952, assistance from other states totaled 102,000,000 DM. In the next two years, the figures were 116,000,000 DM and 144,000,000 DM.[63] The present arrangements for horizontal equalization are governed by the law of 1959 which prescribes a complicated formula for determining the paying and the receiving states.[64] For the fiscal year 1958-1959, the Länder making payments to other Länder were Baden-Württemberg, Bremen, Hamburg, Hesse, and North Rhine–Westphalia; the Länder receiving payments from other Länder were Bavaria, Lower Saxony, Rhineland-Palatinate and Schleswig-Holstein.[65] The definitive payments and receipts were as follows.

	DM Paid
Baden-Württemberg	119,660,000
Bremen	11,042,000
Hamburg	265,210,000
Hesse	72,178,000
North Rhine–Westphalia	486,590,000

	DM Received
Bavaria	220,308,000
Lower Saxony	266,804,000
Rhineland-Palatinate	224,626,000
Schleswig-Holstein	242,948,000

"Bear ye one another's burdens" seems to be a maxim of federalism, but it is not one which is universally popular either in the wealthier states of the United States or in West Germany. The "undeveloped areas" within a federal system thus pose a persistent and difficult problem of intergovernmental financial relations.

4 STATE SELF-GOVERNMENT: GENERAL ASPECTS

In the previous chapter, the question was raised, "Do the states have any significant authority which they can exercise at their own discretion, or are they merely ministerial agents of the Bund?" This is a matter which requires further examination beyond what has already been made. Some Germans have answered the question in terms of the latter alternative. In a Hessian Landtag budget debate, a speaker argued that the Landtag is of little importance because the Länder have lost their character as states. "The more they become administrative provinces (*Verwaltungsprovinzen*) of the Bund, the less will be the political function of the Landtag."[1] At about the same time, a newspaper contributor asserted that state legislative work is trifling, because most substantive laws within the competence of the Länder have now been enacted in more or less permanent form.[2] Before these criticisms can be properly assessed, the nature and scope of state discretion must be analyzed in some detail.

Although in one sense the states are administrative agents of the Bund, they are far from being robots. In performing this major role, they have much influence in determining what the federal law shall be which they administer. Federal ministries usually consult their counterparts in the Länder when drafting statutes. When bills are introduced in the Parliament, the states, through the Bundesrat, often make their views prevail. After enactment, state implementing legislation may be necessary, as well as federal administrative regulations which require Bundesrat approval. As it operates today, the agency role of the Länder is a two-way street.

Of course, if state self-government under federalism is to have much reality, it must mean more than agency. It must involve at least three other characteristics. In the first place, as will be explained later, the constituent units must have a number of important functions which they can undertake independently of the federal government. These functions may be handled by each state acting for itself or, as will be shown in the next paragraphs, two or more states may jointly promote them. Secondly, the Länder must have some taxes which they can levy and spend at their own discretion, a situation which is provided for in Article 106-2 of the *Grundgesetz*. Finally, they must have a large measure of freedom in determining their own constitutions, governmental structures and processes.

INTERSTATE COOPERATION

In addition to that which is institutionalized in the Bundesrat, the West German Länder engage in numerous types of formal and informal interstate cooperation. Cooperation is greater than in the United States. It is facilitated because there are only ten states instead of fifty; the Länder are more homogeneous than the American commonwealths; and they are all staffed by professional bureaucracies who "speak the same language" and are accustomed to working with each other.

According to Neunreither,[3] there are eighty-three interstate organizations or committees of one kind or another in which the states participate. The ministers-president have long been meeting together to discuss common problems,[4] and so do other state officials.[5] For example, there is a "Permanent Conference of Ministers of Education"; and the same pattern holds for the Land ministers who are concerned with housing. Beginning in 1956, various Germans, who committed crimes against the German penal code during the Hitler regime, have been tried in the courts and sentenced to prison. At the annual conference of Land ministers of justice in October 1958, it was decided to set up a central office in Ludwigsburg, Württemberg-Baden, to facilitate cooperation between the states in prosecuting these cases.[6]

More formal interstate action is exemplified by treaties (*Staatsverträge*) and administrative agreements (*Verwaltungsabkommen*) between the Länder. Between 1949 and 1957, more than three hundred such pacts were concluded.[7] Some of these related to police matters such as the Northwest German *Polizeiabkommen*.[8] Others were concerned with radio broadcasting or with certain specialized schools. Lower Saxony and Schleswig-Holstein have a common supreme administrative court (*Oberverwaltungsgericht*) serving both states, while Bremen, Hamburg, and Schleswig-Holstein have provided that the *Landgericht* of Hamburg will have jurisdiction over patent cases in the tristate area. All the Länder are parties to an agreement fixing the distribution of the proceeds of the fire protection tax (*Feuerschutzsteuer*). While most of the numerous illustrations which may be cited are not of great intrinsic importance, they do demonstrate the possibilities of interstate compacts, particularly in fields such as education which are reserved to the Länder.

STATE ADMINISTRATION

Do the Länder have a large measure of discretion in determining their own constitutions, governmental structures and processes? It has already been shown that this is the case with constitutions, election methods, cabinets and legislatures. But how is it in administration? Do the states enjoy substantial autonomy in matters relating to administrative organization, personnel, and budgeting?

In a federal system having both vertical and horizontal

financial equalization, no state has unlimited control over its own budget, although it may influence the equalization formulas through its votes in the Bundesrat. Nevertheless, there is a state budget which is voted by the Landtag with some freedom of choice.

Civil Service

With respect to personnel, the states are subject to a number of federal constitutional and legislative limitations. In view of the role of the Länder in executing federal laws, these, for the most part, are appropriate. For example, Article 33 of the *Grundgesetz* prescribes the traditional principles of the professional civil service for all levels of government.[9] This is more sweeping than in the United States where Congress has required "merit" systems for certain state programs receiving federal grants-in-aid.

In this connection, it may be mentioned that, unlike the situation in the Weimar Republic, professional civil servants now expect and accept policy guidance from those holding political positions. Moreover, within the higher ranks of the civil service, appointments and promotions are not always made without reference to political considerations.[10]

More controversial is Article 131, which represents the German reaction to the fiasco of Allied denazification policy,[11] and which in turn may justly be criticized for undue leniency to civil servants who "went along" with Hitler. The article was implemented by a federal statute of 1951[12] which has been strictly rather than broadly interpreted by the Federal Constitutional Court.[13]

The act of 1951 directed the restoration of pension rights or the reinstatement in office of all former officials, except those who had been permanently disqualified by the denazification courts (a relatively small number), or whose original appointment had been made by the National Socialist regime, or whose only service was in the secret police

(GESTAPO). The law also extended the same right to former civil servants who were expellees or refugees from the East. State and local governments (except *Gemeinden* with populations of 3,000 or less) were required to fill 20 percent of their positions with unemployed refugee officials or officials from defunct administrative agencies.[14] According to Schultes,[15] the effect of Article 131 and its implementing legislation was to take over from 60 to 70 percent of the officials who had served under the Hitler regime.

As the years pass and the so-called "131'ers" die off, Article 131 will decrease in significance. In fairness to the West Germans, it should also be noted that a second law of 1951 offered similar restitution to former officials who had been dismissed or who had otherwise suffered under Nazi rule.

Of greater permanent effect is the federal "framework" legislation (*Rahmenvorschriften*) authorized under Article 75-1. This gives the Bund the right to establish general principles concerning the legal relations of persons in state and local government service.[16]

Between 1955 and 1957, three important federal statutes were enacted which largely unified civil service principles for all levels of government. The first of these is the Personnel Representation Act.[17] This provides a kind of British Whitley Council scheme of advisory representative committees elected by those in the public service and concerned with the issuance of service regulations and the handling of grievances.[18] The second is the Federal Salary Act dealing with salaries and fringe benefits.[19] Finally, there is the Framework Law for the Unification of Civil Service Law.

These federal measures do not immediately bind the states but they do require them, within prescribed periods of time, to pass laws embodying the federally enunciated principles. For example, Chapter III of the Federal Salary Act, which contains the *Rahmenvorschriften,* does not directly fix state salary schedules but it does lay down ratios and percentages which the Länder must follow as between different personnel grades. The legislation just described was long in the making and involved much discussion and negotiation between the Bund, the states and the organized associations of local governments. The Länder may not be the sole authors of the rules governing their civil service establishments but they may fairly be called co-authors.[20]

"Verwaltungsautonomie"

The administrative organization of the Länder comprises, not only the state hierarchy of central, district, and local offices, but also the basic local authorities such as counties and municipalities. As previously indicated, the Bund uses the Länder for the execution of many federal laws. Similarly, the states rely upon the local units to carry out much state and federal legislation. Although local government will be examined later, it may be noted here that it belongs to state and not to federal or concurrent jurisdiction. Subject to the constitutional guarantees of local self-government, the states have full control of it.

Apart from uniform principles embodied in personnel legislation, federal supervision or control of state administration shows considerable variation from one function to another. It is greatest in delegated administration (*Auftragsverwaltung*), as is illustrated by Articles 85, 89 and 90 of the Constitution.[21] In most instances, however, according to the theory of the *Grundgesetz*, state control of administration ("*Verwaltungsautonomie*") is the rule. Articles 83 and 84-1 read:

> The states execute federal laws as matters of their own concern (*landeseigene Verwaltung*) insofar as this *Grundgesetz* does not otherwise provide or permit.
> If the states execute federal laws as matters of their own concern, they determine their administrative structure and procedure insofar as federal laws approved by the Bundesrat do not otherwise provide.

Although *"Verwaltungsautonomie"* is the theory, the exceptions are numerous in practice; it is sometimes charged that the exceptions have become the rule,[22] and that the term itself has become obsolete.[23] For example, the so-called "Expellee Charter" of 1953 commands the Länder to establish central state refugee administrations to execute the law.[24] However, such expansionist tendencies of the Bund can always be prevented by a Bundesrat veto when state cabinets feel strongly about the *"Verwaltungsautonomie"* of the Länder.

In the United States during the twentieth century, the question of state administrative reorganization has been extensively studied. The volume of official and unofficial recommendations concerning the problem is large but the actual achievements thus far are relatively small.

All this is familiar in the West German Länder where there is a considerable literature on *Verwaltungsreform*.[25] The term is a broad one. Among other things, it includes reduction in the number of state ministries; revision of the basic local government statutes such as the *Gemeindeordnungen* and *Kreisordnungen* (now substantially completed); and consolidation of local units (hardly touched because of the political implications). There are still too many small rural counties in Bavaria just as there are too many in the American state of Georgia.[26]

Verwaltungsreform is also concerned with the government district (*Regierungsbezirk*), something which has no parallel in the American commonwealths. It is the intermediate level or focus (*Mittelinstanz, Mittelstufe*) of state administration, standing between the central ministries of the Land on the one hand and the state agencies at county level on the other. The *Regierungsbezirk* has been important historically, particularly in Prussian territories. It exists today in the six largest Länder,[27] ranging in number from three in Hesse to eight in Lower Saxony.[28]

The *Regiergungsbezirk* is not a unit of local self-government; it is an area or district of general state administration, headed by a state-appointed *Regierungspräsident*. As in the pre-Hitler period, the *Regierungspräsident* is still a key official with a large staff.[29] He is charged with important responsibilities relating to police, the supervison of local governments, secondary education, highways, etc. He is, however, more closely controlled by the state cabinet than was the case before 1933.

Do the small states of West Germany really need a *Mittelinstanz* for the execution of their functions? All the Länder, except Bavaria (27,239 square miles) are smaller than West Virginia (24,181 square miles) which ranks forty-first in area among the American states. In spite of considerable controversy about the question,[30] state legislation has, on the whole, confirmed the traditional pattern of the *Regierungsbezirk*.[31]

POLICE

Like the United States Constitution, the *Grundgesetz* does not specifically enumerate the functions reserved to the Länder. But topics not mentioned in the long lists of exclusive and concurrent legislative powers are presumed to be under state jurisdiction. While the sphere is less broad than that enjoyed by America's fifty commonwealths, it nevertheless exists as an important hallmark of federalism.[32] In this category, the most important subjects are: the Land governmental and administrative structure (already covered in the previous discussion) ; the police system; local government; and cultural affairs.

With reference to police, the Bund does have a certain jurisdiction. Attention has already been called to the Federal Criminal Police Office and the Federal Office for the Protection of the Constitution. The Bund may enact general principles concerning the registration and identity cards which all West Germans must carry. The Border Police (*Bundesgrenzschutz*) under the Federal Ministry of the Interior may also be mentioned. But while the Land minister of the interior is the top police official in his state, the role of the Federal Minister of the Interior is hardly comparable.

May the Bund act in police matters reserved to the Länder? In 1951, Parliament passed the *Jugendschutzgesetz*,[33] a law for the protection of youth in public places and amusement establishments. Since the *Grundgesetz* does not mention *Jugendrecht* or *Polizeirecht* among the concurrent powers, this legislation has been criticized as beyond the powers of the Bund.[34] The Federal Minister of the Interior, Gerhard Schröder, strongly believes that federal police power should be enlarged.[35] His bill to implement the emergency police powers envisaged by Article 91 of the Constitution has met with strong opposition.[36]

In spite of these real or threatened encroachments, the police sphere still belongs mainly to the Länder. It is centrally directed and controlled by the Land minister of the interior, although administration may be delegated to local authorities.[37] American and British efforts in the early postwar years to decentralize or municipalize police systems have by this time largely been discarded in favor of the traditional pattern.[38]

Thus in Baden-Württemberg, where there had previously been many municipal systems, the law of 1955 made police matters an exclusive state function.[39] However, the act did permit cities with more than 75,000 inhabitants to petition the minister of the interior for municipal systems. Only Stuttgart, Mannheim, Karlsruhe, and Pforzheim did so—in spite of the fact that this action was disadvantageous to them in terms of state financial assistance in police administration.[40]

During the past decade, much significant state police legislation has been enacted. These laws have drawn extensively upon the Prussian *Polizeiverwaltungsgesetz* of 1931, in its day an exceptionally enlightened statute.[41]

LOCAL GOVERNMENT

One of the main fields under state jurisdiction is local government. The doctrine of local self-government (*Kommunalselbstverwaltung*),[42] proclaimed by Baron vom Stein after Prussia's great defeat at Jena in 1806, is today specifically affirmed by federal and state constitutional provisions. Article 28 of the *Grundgesetz* reads:

> . . . *Gemeinden* must be guaranteed the right to regulate, under their own responsibility and within the limits of the laws, all the affairs of the local community. *Gemeindeverbände* also have the rights of self-government in accordance with the laws, within the limits of the functions given to them by law.

Local Units

The basic and historic local unit is the *Gemeinde* (municipality or commune) which, in area and population, may range from the small rural hamlet with its surrounding fields and farms to the large city.[43] The more populous *Gemeinden* generally have the legal title of "*Stadt*" (city). If the number of inhabitants attains a prescribed minimum (the requirements varying from state to state), the city may become a *Stadtkreis*, that is, a "city-county" or, in the English terminology, "county-borough." The *Stadtkreis* is detached governmentally from the county in which it is geographically situated and is freed from supervision by the county authorities.[44] Other *Gemeinden*, whether classed as cities or not, remain under county supervision.[45]

The *Gemeinden,* whether urban or rural in their social and economic composition, are general purpose units of local self-government. They constitute the base of the governmental pyramid. Above them are the *Gemeindeverbände* which are unions or associations of *Gemeinden* with functions defined by law.

The principal type of *Gemeindeverband* covered by Article 28 of the *Grundgesetz* is the *Landkreis* (rural county), which was a nineteenth-century creation, uniting all the *kreisangehörige Gemeinden* within the county area.[46] It is called a "rural county" to distinguish it from the "city-county" which is a city exercising county as well as municipal functions. Since the average size of the *Landkreis* is less than that of the British or American county, some county consolidation would be desirable, but this is politically difficult to achieve—just as it is in the United States.

Therefore, when the county area is too small or otherwise inappropriate for certain functions, there is a tendency to create a special authority (*Zweckverband*) for the region concerned. In some instances, the Land and the Bund may also be members. There are over five thousand *Zweckverbände* in the Bundesrepublik, the oldest and best known being the Regional Planning Federation of the Ruhr Coal Mining District, created in 1920.[47]

In several states, such as North Rhine–Westphalia, Rhineland-Palatinate and Schleswig-Holstein, there is a smaller kind of *Gemeindeverband* known as the *Amt.* Instead of being countywide, the *Amt* unites several small neighboring *Gemeinden.*

Above the county level, there are a few units of local self-government, three examples of which may be cited. The *Landeswohlfahrtsverband Hessen* is a statewide consolidation which replaces three regional units in Hesse. The *Landeskommunalverband des Hohenzollernschen Landes* in

Baden-Württemberg is the old Prussian enclave of Hohenzollern. The third illustration is from North Rhine–Westphalia.

When that state was formed, there was some discontent in the former province of Westphalia where people felt they had been annexed by the Rhine province. Both the state capital, Düsseldorf, and the federal capital, Bonn, are in Rhine province areas. The old provincial self-government was missed. Because of Westphalian opinion, the Landtag in 1953 created two large, regional self-governing units (*Landschaftsverbände*), one for Westphalia-Lippe and the other for the North Rhine area. Each of these has a representative assembly modelled on the old Prussian *Provinziallandtag*.[48]

Various internal structural and operational aspects of local units will not be treated here.[49] However, it may be said in passing that, during the past decade, the state legislatures have done good work in enacting permanent basic statutes relating to local government, particularly the Municipal Government Acts (*Gemeindeordnungen*) and the County Government Acts (*Kreisordnungen* or *Landkreisordnugen*).[50] The passage of these laws has usually been preceded by lengthy committee and plenary session deliberations in which all points of view have had an opportunity to be heard. For example, the legislative discussion of the Lower Saxony *Landkreisordnung* of 1958 took two and a half years.[51]

Intergovernmental Relations

Although local government structure and operations are intentionally not stressed in the present study, the local units have intergovernmental relations with each other and with the higher levels, the Land and the Bund. These require examination, especially the state-local and the federal-local patterns. Before commenting upon these "vertical" types, something more should be said about "horizontal" examples.

Some of the latter have already been mentioned, such as the interrelations of local units in *Zweckverbände*. While the Landkreis stands above its constituent *Gemeinden* so that the relation is not strictly "horizontal," it is still inter-local in character. Another "horizontal" illustration is afforded by the associations or unions of local authorities, the so-called *Kommunalspitzenverbände*.[52] In an age of organized pressure groups, cities and counties, whether in the United States or in West Germany, also need to be united for dealing with state and federal executives and legislatures and for discussion of common problems among themselves.

Although the Hanover *Städteverein* was founded as early as 1866, the year in which the Kingdom of Hanover was annexed by Prussia, it was not until after 1900 that nation-wide associations came into existence. The most powerful of these is the *Deutscher Städtetag*, established in 1905 with headquarters in Cologne; it is the *Spitzenverband* of the larger cities, particularly the *Stadtkreise*.[53] The association of the rural counties, the *Deutscher Landkreistag* with headquarters in Bonn, dates from 1920.[54] The smaller cities have the *Deutscher Städtebund* (1910) in Düsseldorf; and for the *Gemeinden* which are not cities, there is the *Deutscher Gemeindetag* (1916) in Bad Godesberg. Because federal policies and financing so much affect local governments, the four associations have formed a joint agency, the *Bundesvereinigung der kommunalen Spitzenverbände* with headquarters in Cologne.

According to the *Bundesvereinigung*, about 75 percent of all federal statutes have direct practical significance for the *Gemeinden*.[55] This does not mean that the Bund by-passes the Länder and makes laws directly for local units. Local government is reserved to the states, a principle which can be defended by Bundesrat veto. Moreover, federal legislation affecting the local authorities cannot ordinarily be applied to them without prior Landtag action.

Historically, the states have delegated to the local units the execution of many of the laws which they have adopted on their own initiative. The same process happens today with federal measures administered by the Länder. The majority of the statutes which the *Gemeinden* now carry out are ultimately federal in character.[56] But it must first be implemented by state legislation determining if and how the local governments will be used by the Länder in fulfilling their federal assignments.

Turning again to the *Grundgesetz*, local government is mentioned or assumed, not only in Article 28 but also in several other places, notably in Articles 75-1, 90, 108, and 131. Moreover, the constitutional amendments on the *Lastenausgleich* (Article 120a) and on military defense (Article 87b) make possible the participation of the *Gemeinden* in *Bundesauftragverwaltung*.[57] Indeed, the 1957 federal civil defense legislation, which was approved by the Bundesrat, provides one of the few illustrations of by-passing the Länder.[58]

It is sometimes denied that there is anything significant left of the *Kommunalselbstverwaltung* guaranteed by Article 28. What that provision aims to secure is only a legal type of organization. The nineteenth-century conception of local self-government is not applicable to the interdependent and highly complex economic and social conditions of the twentieth century.

As defenders of local "home rule," the *Kommunalspitzenverbände* do not accept this interpretation of Article 28.[59] They admit that "things are not what they used to be." Whatever the sphere of independent municipal action in the past, it has been greatly circumscribed by the growth of delegated (and hence mandatory) functions, and by the distribution of costs and revenues among levels of government. Nevertheless, they contend that local units still have *"eigene Angelegenheiten."*

In the final analysis, the crux of *Kommunalselbstverwaltung* is finance. Both in the United States and in West Germany, the local authorities have fared badly in the scramble for funds. With American state lawmakers indifferent or hostile, the organized local governments, particularly the cities, have turned increasingly to Washington for help. A similar pattern can be observed in the Bundesrepublik, although in general the legislatures of the Länder have better records than their American counterparts. Just as the Federal Parliament passes finance equalization laws dealing with federal-state financial relations, so also each Landtag must do the same for state-local financial relations, which include state payments to local governments.

Since some Länder are rich and others are poor, state aid to local government shows great variations. In the fiscal year 1957-1958, figuring the per capita average on the basis of the entire population of the state, a pronounced "spread" was noted. In North Rhine–Westphalia, state payments to the *Gemeinden* amounted to 100.07 DM per capita; but in Rhineland-Palatinate, the corresponding figure was only 35.38 DM per capita.[60] Such state legislation naturally arouses great debate and is frequently amended.

The complaints of the *Kommunalspitzenverbände* may be summarized as follows:[61]

1. Delegated functions are increasing but without the local governments being fully reimbursed for the expenditures which they incur in connection with these mandatory obligations.

2. The taxes which may be locally levied are too few in number and do not yield adequate revenues.

3. In the period of postwar reconstruction and expansion, municipalities have had to make heavy capital outlays for

hospitals, schools, streets and a variety of other public in-
stallations, most of which are not directly revenue-produc-
ing. Since these could not be financed out of current funds,
the money was borrowed. Consequently, in the decade 1949-
1959, the *Gemeinden* accumulated an indebtedness of almost 11 billion DM, a figure higher than it was before
World War II.[62]

In 1932, a German scholar and official wrote, "It is wrong
to speak of priority of financial need and urgency among
levels of government in terms of a series which puts the
Reich first; the Länder second; and the *Gemeinden* last."[63]
This doctrine is fully accepted by the organized local governments. Since Article 28 of the *Grundgesetz* guarantees *Kommunalselbstverwaltung*, it should also contain a financial
guarantee as a corollary. The local authorities should be
recognized as financial partners with the Bund and the
Länder and the needs of each evaluated in the light of the
total governmental responsibilities for the national welfare.
In this way, they argue, the ideal of a three-layered federal
state *(ein dreigeschichteter Bundesstaat)* may be realized.[64]
In other words, what the West German associations of local
units are advocating is "cooperative federalism" with close
federal-state-local ties.

The *Kommunalspitzenverbände* have, therefore, pressed
for constitutional amendment relating to the intergovernmental division of revenues. Their goal was partly accomplished in 1955 and 1956, the 1956 amendment reading
as follows:[65]

Article 106-6. The yield from the real estate and business
taxes *(Realsteuern)* belongs to the *Gemeinden*. . . . From
the state share in the yield from the income and corporation
tax, there accrues to the *Gemeinden* and *Gemeindeverbände*
collectively a prescribed percentage determined by state
law. As for the other state taxes, the state determines if and
how far the yield from these accrues to the *Gemeinden* and
Gemeindeverbände.

Article 107-7. If in the areas of particular states or local governments, the Bund creates special establishments which cause more direct expenditures or less income to the governments in question, the Bund will guarantee the necessary equalization if and insofar as the state and local governments cannot be expected to bear the special burden. . . .[66]

While the changes just cited are not the full partnership desired, they are a move in the right direction. Whatever steps may subsequently be taken, it is certain that the organized local authorities will continue to have much to say about federal-state-local relations in general and financial relations in particular.[67]

5 STATE SELF-GOVERNMENT: CULTURAL AFFAIRS

To the American tourist in West Germany, the term "cultural affairs" may suggest theaters, opera houses, museums, libraries, and historic buildings. Most of these structures are government property, belonging to some Land or *Gemeinde*, or are publicly subsidized. Historically, the support of these undertakings was an important part of state and local self-government; and the same is true today. Indeed, it was sometimes said that, when the Germans had to decide between a government housing program and the rebuilding of a state or municipal theater which had been destroyed by bombs, they chose the latter.

For the people of the Federal Republic, "cultural affairs" means more than what has just been suggested. Among other things, it includes mass communications media, education, and religion. These three areas and most other aspects of cultural affairs fall within the domain of the Länder.

THE BUND AND CULTURAL AFFAIRS

Although the Bill of Rights of the *Grundgesetz* contains articles relating to education, religion, and opinion-forming media, these are almost wholly absent from the catalogue of federal legislative jurisdiction. In the list of concurrent subjects, the Bund may legislate to protect German cultural treasures against removal abroad (Article 74-5), and to promote scientific research (Article 74-13).[1]

In 1958, there was established the Scientific Council (*Wissenschaftsrat*) as an advisory coordinating group representing the Bund, the states and private organizations. The Council was created by an administrative agreement between the federal and state governments. When the agreement was signed in September 1957, Chancellor Adenauer stated that it "involves—I want particularly to emphasize this—the introduction of no centralistic scientific policy."[2]

In addition to the promotion and financing of scientific research, the Bund also provides services and funds in other sectors of the cultural field.[3] Thus the Federal Ministry for All-German Affairs helps finance school construction in the endangered Eastern frontier regions of the West German Republic.[4] The Federal Ministry for Family and Youth Affairs is small in staff and budget but it has been criticized as a threat to the powers reserved to the Länder.

More important in the cultural field is the Federal Ministry of the Interior. It has a division on "Cultural Affairs of the Bund" which is interested in promotion of the arts and sciences; school questions; press, radio and film; and similar matters. Likewise under the Ministry of the Interior is the Central Office for Internal Information (*Bundeszentrale für Heimatdienst*).[5] It is an important agency for the defense of democracy and the spirit of European union against subversive attacks from the Right and from the Left. The *Bundeszentrale* concentrates on schools, and on youth and civic organizations, providing financial support for the latter if they contribute at least half of their own expenses. It has a substantial publication program, including such periodicals as *Information zur politischen Bildung, Staatsbürgerliche Informationen*, and *Das Parlament*.

Although the *"Kulturhoheit"* of the Länder has often been threatened by federal expansionist tendencies which have provoked controversies with the states,[6] the sphere of Land jurisdiction has, on the whole, been successfully defended. Today, it is widely, although far from universally, accepted.

MASS COMMUNICATIONS MEDIA

The Press

In a mature Western democracy such as Britain, the role of mass communications media[7] is well established. Government policy and administration are unusually sensitive to public opinion as formulated or reflected through these channels. By comparison, the Bundesrepublik has not yet become a second Britain. Nevertheless, the situation today is strikingly different from what prevailed during the Hitler regime; it is also more than just a restoration of pre-1933 conditions.[8]

The Nazi tyranny introduced a highly centralized government and party control of information. Developments since 1945 have stressed decentralization of public authority in this field, together with more adequate constitutional guarantees of liberty in what individuals and groups may speak, print, and disseminate. In part, this has been the natural German reaction to what the nation experienced under the Third Reich. In the *Grundgesetz,* Article 5 of the Bill of Rights is a marked improvement over the corresponding provisions of the Weimar Constitution. In part, it is due to reforms made by the Western occupying powers.[9] Allied efforts with respect to information media have had more positive and more enduring results than their endeavors in other areas such as punishment of war criminals, denazification, and civil service.

In the federal-state division of powers, governmental regulation is largely vested in the Länder. Although the Bund, according to Article 75-2 of the *Grundgesetz,* may constitutionally enact principles (*Rahmenvorschriften*) concerning the general legal relations of press and film, there has thus far been no implementation of the provision.

On a number of occasions, the Federal Cabinet has unsuccessfully urged various measures relating to information matters. Thus the press bill of 1952, drafted by the Federal Ministry of the Interior, aroused so much objection that it was never submitted to Parliament.[10] In 1953, 1954, and 1957, futile attempts were made to establish central office control over the press relations of federal agencies.[11]

In 1953, the Federal Cabinet did manage to secure the enactment of the "smut" law (*Schmutz- und Schundgesetz*) which was designed to protect youth from publications glorifying crime and immorality.[12] It prohibited the exhibition, advertisement, and sale of such "trash" to persons under eighteen years of age. The bill met opposition in Parliament and from most of the German press. It was pointed out that a similar statute had been enacted under the Weimar Republic and had been repealed two years later. Moreover, the bill was unnecessary because the German Criminal Code had for many years forbidden the sale of obscene and pornographic literature to minors. Although the measure was adopted, that did not end the story. The administration of the law, with its black lists and confiscations, has given rise to charges of censorship and arbitrary action.[13]

Turning from the federal to the state level, in the early years of the occupation, the German press operated under military government licenses. On September 30, 1948, the United States Military Governor, General Lucius D. Clay, issued a memorandum announcing that the licensing power would be relinquished as soon as the states in the American areas of control adopted satisfactory laws guaranteeing the freedom of the press. Such legislation must:[14]

1. Implement the general guarantees of a free press as expressed in the state constitutions, and exclude any system of special licensing not required of all other business enterprises.

2. Protect the press from governmental domination or domination by special interests.

3. Guarantee the prerogatives of a free press in obtaining and publishing information of public interest.

4. Guarantee that there be no arbitrary interference by the police or other administrative bodies in the free flow and dissemination of news and printed matter.

5. Specifically exclude the revival of honor courts, press chambers or other forms of organized press control exercised by the Nazi regime.

6. Prohibit censorship or control of the content of news and published material except through legal process in the event of a violation of existing laws regarding libel, defamation, fraud, indecency or breach of the peace.

It took about a year's time and much argument before statutes which military government regarded as "satisfactory" were adopted by Bavaria, Bremen, Hesse, and Württemberg-Baden. In the British and French zones of occupation, the termination of licensing was accomplished by military government decree but without as much prescription of future standards as in the American areas. Hence the former British and French zone Länder usually revived, with a few changes, the Reich Press Law of 1934 which in turn was based on the original federal statute of 1874. There is, however, an important difference, emphasized by the Federal Constitutional Court in a 1958 decision. The Court held that such parts of the old Reich Press Law as are still in force are now state and not federal law.[15] With the passage of Allied High Commission Law No. 5 on September 21, 1949,[16] previous American, British, and French military government legislation relating to press and censorship was repealed.[17]

The federal uniformity of the Bismarckian Empire and of the Weimar Republic has thus been replaced by the state diversity of the Bundesrepublik. This has its advantages but it can also mean that the law of one state is less satisfactory than that of another when measured by General Clay's criteria. There is a difference between the statute of Hesse which specifies that, in order to confiscate the issue of a newspaper or periodical, a court order is first needed; and certain other state statutes which permit the police to confiscate, the court proceedings following thereafter. Some cases of confiscations have occurred within the territories of the Federal Republic—and not just seizures of Communist publications after that party was declared unconstitutional by the Federal Constitutional Court. For example, the sensational weekly periodical, *Der Spiegel,* published in Hamburg, can be very provocative; on occasion, it has been too provocative for the authorities.[18]

In spite of these shortcomings, the outlook is hopeful. Allied reforms in the information field have acquired much German support. In contrast with earlier practices, the West German record in maintaining a free press has, on the whole, been good.

Radio and Television

Like the press, the organizational pattern of radio and television continues to exhibit the effects of Allied decentralizing policies.[19] Until the end of the World War II, these media were centralized under the Reich Post Office. The occupying powers broke up this tight monopoly, each zone going its own way. British military government established a single zonal radio network modelled after the British Broadcasting Corporation; the same was done in the French zone. American military government organized a radio system in each of its four states. The situation thus created was, for all practical purposes, "frozen" by Allied High Commission Law No. 5.[20] It remained so until 1955 when West Germany gained sovereignty and the Allied High Commission was abolished.

Since then, there have been a few changes. In 1955, the British-initiated zonal network was divided between two companies, the *Westdeutscher Rundfunk* and the *Nord-*

deutscher Rundfunk. Excluding Radio Free Berlin in West Berlin,[21] there are at present seven German broadcasting corporations in the Federal Republic, namely: West German Radio (Cologne) ; North German Radio (Hamburg) ; Radio Bremen; Hessian Radio (Frankfurt); Bavarian Radio (Munich) ; South German Radio (Stuttgart) ; and Saarland Radio (Saarbrücken) . In addition to the main stations just listed, each network usually has a number of smaller stations.

As required by military government directives, these companies are organized by state legislation in the form of autonomous public law corporations *(Anstalten des öffentlichen Rechts)* . Since the North German Radio serves three states (Hamburg, Lower Saxony, Schleswig-Holstein), it rests upon a "treaty" *(Staatsvertrag)* between them.[22] When the British-sponsored Northwest German Radio was replaced by the West and North German Radios, a liquidation treaty was concluded between the four Länder concerned (North Rhine–Westphalia, Hamburg, Lower Saxony, Schleswig-Holstein) .[23]

The liquidation treaty also created the *Nord- und Westdeutscher Rundfunkverband* as a partnership of the two companies for television. Television was not revived in West Germany until December 1952. Because of the great expense involved, television is handled as a joint program of all seven broadcasting corporations, which have appointed a "Coordinator of German Television." There is a single channel providing a daily program over thirty television transmitters.[24]

While the broadcasting corporations operate with a large measure of independence from state government, they do not all have the same internal structure. In the South German Radio, the supervisory council *(Aufsichtsrat)* functions as a kind of board of directors and is widely representative. Most of its members are named by organized groups (religious, educational, labor, chamber of commerce, journalists, publishers, etc.) with only five members elected by the Baden-Württemberg Landtag. The *Aufsichtsrat* supervises program policy and appoints the director. There is also a smaller administrative council (*Verwaltungsrat*) made up of five persons chosen by the supervisory council and four by the Landtag.

In contrast, the West German Radio has a different organizational framework. The supervisory council is entirely elected by the Landtag of North Rhine–Westphalia in such a way as to give proportional representation to the political parties having seats in the legislature. The supervisory council elects a program advisory board and a smaller administrative council; the latter appoints the director.

With radio and television under Land jurisdiction, what, if any, authority is left to the Bund? Under Article 73-7, of the *Grundgesetz,* the Bund has exclusive legislative power over postal and telecommunication services and these are directly administered by a federal ministry. Although "telecommunications" do not include radio and television, the ministry does have a role as a collecting agency. Prior to 1945, radio broadcasting was financed by fees from the owners of receiving sets which were collected by the Reichspost. The Bundespost in West Germany has succeeded to this function. The monthly license fee amounts to 2 DM for a radio set and 7 DM for a television set. However, if an individual has both types of sets, he pays only 7 DM. After the Post Office has deducted a small collection charge, the balance is turned over to the broadcasting corporations and constitutes their principal source of income. Recently, a very small amount of commercial advertising has been introduced which, in the case of television, amounts to a maximum of four minutes between 7:00 and 8:00 P.M.[25]

Since the assignment of frequencies among nations may involve international agreements, the Bund controls the allocation of frequencies within West Germany. This can be a weapon in federal-state controversies over radio and television. When in 1959 the broadcasting corporations talked about setting up a second joint television program in addition to the one which they already had, the Federal Minister of Posts and Telecommunications said that he would refuse to grant the necessary frequencies.[26]

The Bund itself does some broadcasting over the *"Deutsche Welle."* This is a short-wave transmission abroad which, by agreement with the North German Radio, uses its facilities in Hamburg[27] On West German territory, there are several foreign radio stations, which broadcast eastward to the Communist orbit. The Voice of America, with its relay base in Munich, is a United States Government enterprise, resting upon bilateral agreement between the two countries. On the other hand, Radio Free Europe and Radio Liberation, located in Munich, are owned and operated by private groups under license from the Federal Republic. The two latter stations have aroused considerable official and unofficial German criticism; from time to time, there has been talk of revoking their licenses.[28]

The main dissatisfaction, however, is not here but with the existing setup of German radio and television. In addition to the arguments about program content and the limited time allowed for advertising, difficult questions are posed by the present method of financing. There are now about four million television sets and over fifteen million radio sets in West Germany and West Berlin.[29] The sets are unequally distributed over the country. Populous and wealthy North Rhine–Westphalia has the greatest number and hence the West German Radio is well-off financially from the fees which it receives. On the other hand, Radio Bremen, because of its limited area and population, does not have enough "paying customers." Were it not for state pride, Bremen might be the fourth Land partner in the North German Radio in the rival port of Hamburg. Similarly, there might be a single corporation for the states of Southwest Germany just as the North German Radio serves Hamburg, Lower Saxony and Schleswig-Holstein.[30] At one time, there was a financial equalization agreement between the rich and the poor broadcasting corporations. This was terminated, but at a 1959 Conference of Ministers-President, a new *"Finanzausgleich"* was discussed.[31]

On several occasions, the Adenauer Cabinet has unsuccessfully sought federal legislation. It is opposed to a solution based on a treaty between the Bund and the states.[32] A cabinet bill of 1959 proposed to create a public law corporation to operate a second television channel on a commercial basis and also to establish separate noncommercial corporations for long-wave and short-wave broadcasting to supplement the state networks. The bill was unanimously rejected by the Bundesrat.[33] Thus this federal-state issue, which has political implications for government and opposition parties, especially as the Bundestag election of 1961 draws near, remains unsettled.

EDUCATION

The West German public school system ranges from the elementary through the intermediate, secondary and vocational schools to the universities and other institutions of higher learning.[34] Although private schools are guaranteed by the *Grundgesetz* (Article 7-4), they are relatively few in number, employing only 10,000 out of 234,000 full-time teachers below the university level.[35] There are, of course, many other forms of education. Preschool children may be cared for in kindergartens, some of which are municipally operated. But the kindergarten is not a part of the public school system. Similarly, much vocational and apprenticeship training is provided outside of the vocational public schools.[36]

Mention should likewise be made of adult education, whether supplied by political parties, labor unions, youth organizations, or adult education schools *(Volkshochschulen)*. The Bundesrepublik has more than a thousand *Volkshochschulen*.[37] They generally have evening classes and often use public school facilities, but are not in the school system. They are financed from both public and private sources. In addition to registration fees from participants, the *Volkshochschulen* are supported from municipal funds and, since 1953, by grants from some of the Länder.

German schools were widely admired in the nineteenth century. How are they today in the aftermath of Hitlerism and war's destruction? Has West Germany merely restored the pre-1933 models with their good and bad features? Or have there been reform and modernization to meet the needs of the age of automation and atomic energy? Not only in the United States but also in the Federal Republic there is great debate on the methods, content, and objectives of education.[38]

With respect to public funds spent on schools, the present records have not yet equalled those set earlier. In Imperial Germany for the fiscal year 1913-1914, 17.1 percent of all public expenditures was for schools and universities. In 1955-1956, including the large sums spent to reconstruct or replace destroyed schools, the corresponding figure for the Bundesrepublik was 10.2 percent. Stated differently but for the same year, West Germany devoted 3.6 percent of the total national income to schools as compared to 4.5 percent in the Netherlands, 5.2 percent in the United States, and 5.7 percent in Japan.[39]

Federal Action or Interstate Cooperation?

What should be the federal role in education? Since the field is one which historically and constitutionally has been reserved to the states, this is a controversial question both in West Germany and in the United States. In 1958, the Federal Minister of Economics, Ludwig Erhard, published a newspaper article entitled, "The Particularism (*Eigenbrötelei*) of the Länder." He assailed the lack of uniformity among the states in school matters, charged that the Länder were unable to solve the problem through interstate cooperation, and urged the creation of a Federal *Kultus* Ministry.[40]

In reply to Erhard's "cavalry raid" into the territory of *Kulturpolitik,* a member of the Hamburg Cabinet, Senator Hans-Harder Biermann-Ratjen, made a spirited defense of the existing system.[41] The Federal Minister is wrong when he asserts that the Western Allies gave cultural jurisdiction to the Länder so that it might be an apple of discord to weaken Germany. On the contrary, the cultural autonomy of the states dates back to the beginnings of German unification. The Empire and the Weimar Republic were built upon it. The short Nazi interlude was the sole exception to the rule. For historical and contemporary reasons, the Senator opposed the creation of a new bureaucratic army in Bonn controlling the cultural sphere.[42] The two opposing views here set forth are typical of what many other Germans have said for and against the present arrangements.

The *Grundgesetz* is conspicuously silent on federal activities in education. The Bill of Rights contains a few provisions which directly or indirectly relate to the public schools. Of these, Article 7 is particularly important; it declares that "the entire educational system is under the supervision of the state" (*Staat*).[43] The word *"Staat"* in this connection means "Land," as is evidenced by the cross reference to Article 7 found in Article 141. While the Bund, as already noted, does have concurrent jurisdiction in promoting research, it has no legislative authority over schools, not even the power to enact general principles (*Rahmenvorschriften*), which the Reich had under the Weimar Constitution.

Hence the Bund is concerned with education in only peripheral ways. In the federal budget for 1959-1960, 1.8 percent of the money was allocated for educational and cultural activities. On the other hand, the total budgets of all the states except the Saar showed 24.5 percent for the same purposes.[44] The federal appropriations included an item of 41,000,000 DM for the assistance of needy university students.[45] Indirectly, the Bund has a somewhat greater role than the statistics imply. When the Bund makes general and unrestricted allotments to the financially weak state of Schleswig-Holstein, these aid all the functions of that Land, including education.

How much educational uniformity should there be under federalism, especially in the United States and West Germany, where there is widespread internal migration of families resulting in transfer of children from one school system to another? If the Bund had authority to lay down general principles, like the federal *Rahmenvorschriften* for state and local civil service, a certain amount of standardization could be produced.[46] Since this is not the case, the approach must be through interstate cooperation.

With only ten constituent units, it might be supposed that cooperation among the Länder in education would be easy. In fact, it is not, at least so far as state lawmaking is concerned. School questions are among the most controversial and costly with which the Landtag deals; its decisions directly affect the voters as parents or taxpayers or both. When interstate cooperation can be secured by administrative action without new legislation, uniform results are less difficult to achieve. Even here, Land cabinets and ministers of education dare not forget their parliamentary responsibility. In interstate conferences, they may unanimously agree on what ought to be done, but administrative or legislative implementation by the individual states is likely to be less than unanimous.

The principal official agencies of interstate educational

cooperation are: the Conference of Land Ministers-President; the Permanent Conference of Ministers of Education and Cultural Affairs; and the German Committee for the Educational System. In addition there are numerous and varied private and public associations which are interested in school questions. At the university level, one finds the West German Rectors' Conference; the Union of Universities (*Hochschulverband*) ; and the *Verband Deutscher Studentenschaften* which is the union of student self-government councils (*ASTA*) .[47] At lower levels, the School Committee of the *Deutscher Städtetag* should be mentioned as well as teachers' organizations, such as the *Gemeinschaft Deutscher Lehrerverbände* and the *Gewerkschaft Erziehung und Wissenschaft,* the last named a kind of labor union of the elementary school teachers.

The Permanent Conference of Ministers of Education (*Ständige Konferenz der Kultusminister der Länder in der Bundesrepublik*) was established in 1948 and has its headquarters and secretariat in Bonn. Attached to it are three full-time committees: on universities and other institutions of higher learning; on elementary, secondary, and vocational schools; and on cultural matters such as fine arts, museums, libraries, and monuments. In 1958, it was reported that the Conference had formulated and carried through more than eighty agreements and decisions aiming at securing greater uniformity between the states.[48]

The most important of these was embodied in a formal document, the Düsseldorf Agreement of February 17, 1955, which was approved by the Conference of Ministers-President.[49] Indeed, the impetus for this pact came originally from the ministers-president. At their 1954 meeting in Munich, they passed a resolution asking the Conference of Ministers of Education to draft proposals on particular topics where greater uniformity between the states would be desirable.[50]

Among other things, the Düsseldorf Agreement dealt with the minimum number of years of compulsory full-time attendance; the date of the beginning of the school year; the time and duration of vacations; the grading system; and standardization of the *Abitur* certificates and of teachers' certificates so as to secure interstate recognition and thus aid persons moving from one state to another.

For its implementation, the Agreement requires state legislative or administrative action. Except for Bavaria, this has largely been secured. In that state, the school year still begins in the fall rather than in April as in other Länder. There have also been difficulties about the length of the summer vacation.[51] At a meeting held in April 1959, the ministers agreed on a general revision of history teaching which would be designed to fill the gap in young people's knowledge about the Hitler regime.[52] This, too, will not be easy to accomplish.

Neither the ministers of education nor the ministers-president are in a position to do much pioneering in the larger issues of educational policy. For this, one must look to the German Committee for the Educational System (*Deutscher Ausschuss für das Erziehungs- und Bildungswesen*). At the initiative of the Bundestag, the Committee was organized in 1953 to serve as a research and advisory body to the Permanent Conference of Ministers of Education. Its twenty members are named by the Federal Minister of the Interior and the President of the Permanent Conference and are drawn from teachers, university professors, artists, scientists, and other interested persons. The Committee has issued a number of reports and recommendations on various subjects. In 1959, it published a comprehensive plan (*Rahmenplan*) for the reorganization of the elementary and secondary public schools.[53]

The Committee's plan, while drawing upon existing patterns, aims to lessen the traditional class character of German education by lengthening the period of compulsory attendance, and by increasing the opportunities at various stages for gifted children of whatever social and economic background to transfer to secondary schools which prepare for admission to the institutions of higher learning. The old rigidities of the "two-track" system would thus be considerably modified. No longer would almost 80 percent of the pupils, at an early age (ten to twelve years), be shunted into a track which ended with the elementary school at the age of fourteen or fifteen, plus two or four more years in part-time vocational schools.

Since the Committee proposed a middle-of-the-road course, there have been many criticisms both from conservatives and from radical school reformers. In any event, the plan is certain to cost more money—and this too is a problem, especially for the less wealthy states. Hence, simultaneous state action to carry it out will be difficult, if not impossible, at least for the immediate future. But as a goal toward which all states ought to move, this *Rahmenplan* has much to be said in its favor. It remains to be seen whether or not it will result in renewed agitation for a federal constitutional amendment authorizing the Bund to enact *Rahmengesetze*.[54]

State-Local Relations in Education

Since education is a function of the Länder, they have, since 1945, passed much legislation on the subject. However, unlike the basic local government statutes which have now achieved relatively permanent forms, school law is still in flux, causing dispute in Landtag sessions.[55]

While the Permanent Conference of Ministers of Education does try to secure certain kinds of uniformity in the public school system, in other areas, such as administrative organization, appointment of teachers and finance, there is considerable diversity among the Länder. In most of the states, three levels of supervisory agencies exist. At the apex of the pyramid is the ministry of education with its various bureaus. Next comes the intermediate level (*Regierungsbezirk*) with control exercised through the office of the *Regierungspräsident*. At the bottom of the supervisory hierarchy is the county. Here the responsible officers are the county director (*Landrat, Oberkreisdirektor*) in the *Landkreise* and the *Oberbürgermeister* (or *Oberstadtdirektor*) in the *Stadtkreise*. With them are usually associated one or more state-appointed school superintendents (*Oberschulräte*). The intermediate and lower levels operate under instructions from the ministry of education.

Although the universities and almost all other institutions of higher learning are state-created and financed, they are largely self-governing but are subject to inspection by the ministry of education.[56] Some of the secondary schools are under the direct administration of the ministry. For most other schools, state supervision is exercised from the *Regierungsbezirk* and county levels.

Unlike most American commonwealths, the autonomous school corporation, governed by a popularly elected school board and vested with authority to levy school taxes, is unknown in the Bundesrepublik. There are, however, local school committees in charge of buildings and equipment. These are elected by the local legislature, partly from its own membership and from the citizens generally. Some members of the school committee may be chosen by the teachers or by the parents' advisory council (*Elternbeirat*), about which more will be said later. Clergymen are usually represented. Like other committees of the legislature, the school committee may be completely subordinated to that body. Or it may, as in Hesse, have a substantial measure of independence from the local legislature and executive.

With respect to curriculum and the qualifications and appointment of teachers, the state has the dominant role. About 87 percent of the public school teachers are classified as state officials. The remainder are municipal officials,[57] and are chiefly found in schools above the elementary level, particularly vocational and intermediate schools. For such, the municipalities (*Gemeinden*) make the selections within the qualifications and under the procedures established by the state. Do the *Gemeinden* have any voice in the choice of teachers who are state officials? In Rhineland-Palatinate, the answer is emphatically in the negative. In other states, the *Gemeinde* executive may have a right of nomination to the state appointing authority for vacancies in the schools within the municipality. Or the state may propose three candidates from whom the *Gemeinde* must choose. In these and other ways, the state takes account of local wishes in the exercise of its appointing power.

As to finance, the burden is heavy on both state and local governments. In the fiscal year 1955-1956, the Länder (including West Berlin) spent 2,620,000,000 DM for schools, and the local governments, 1,784,000,000 DM.[58] The traditional principle was that the state was responsible for personnel costs (salaries and pensions of teachers) and that the local governments paid the physical costs (erection and maintenance of school buildings). In Rhineland-Palatinate, teachers are still paid exclusively by the state, but elsewhere mixed systems prevail. Teachers who are municipal officials are locally paid. For those who are state officials, local governments are frequently required to pay a portion of the salaries involved.

On the other hand, in cases of need, the state may make grants to local governments for school construction and repair. Indeed, without state help, the bombed-out schools could scarcely have been restored or replaced. There are also other forms of state aid. In the past, tuition was regularly charged in the intermediate and secondary schools, as well as in the universities. Under legislation adopted since 1945, intermediate and secondary tuition fees have either been eliminated or are in the process of being abolished. The state reimburses local governments for the loss of revenue which they thus incur. But even with all the state aid, some *Gemeinden*, especially in rural areas, are too small and too weak financially to provide adequate elementary school buildings. Hence the laws permit neighboring units of this sort to unite in a special authority (*Zweckschulverband*) and thus pool their resources.

From the above account, it is apparent that the local citizens in West Germany have less to say about their schools than is the case in the United States. Various Land constitutions do recognize the rights of parents in the education of their children, but these guarantees are chiefly significant with respect to religious instruction, as will be explained in the next section. Although advisory councils of parents for each school are frequently authorized by law, there are few such bodies which can compare with their vigorous counterparts in many American communities.[59]

Occasionally, fathers and mothers do act. Ten parents in Hesse appealed to the state supreme court because the ministry of education had ordered reforms in the secondary school curriculum without consulting the parents as required by Article 56-6 of the Hesse Constitution. In February 1958, the court invalidated the order. The Landtag thereupon passed a law creating a state advisory council on which parents, teachers and other interested groups were represented.[60]

Education and Religion: Background of the Problem

Both education and religion fall within the sphere of cultural affairs reserved to the Länder. Hence, church-state relations constitute a state rather than a federal problem. Prior to 1933, various Länder had concordats with the

Vatican and "treaties" (*Verträge*) with the Evangelical *Landeskirchen* in their respective areas. In several state constitutions adopted since 1945, these agreements are recognized as continuing in effect.[61] Since then, new agreements have been made in a number of states.[62] Among other things, they contain sections on the financial relations of church and state, such as state subsidies to the churches and the use of government tax machinery for the collection of church taxes from church members.[63] These arrangements are unknown in the United States. Their present existence in the Federal Republic can only be explained historically.

Since the Protestant Reformation, Germany has been divided religiously. Indeed, the principle *"cuius regio eius religio,"* laid down in 1555 by the Peace of Augsburg, may be regarded as an important factor contributing to federalism. In the nineteenth century, thanks to Bismarck's Kulturkampf, the Center or Catholic Party grew to be a leading party in the Empire and remained so under the Weimar Republic.

The persecution of the churches by the Hitler regime drew Catholic and Protestants together so that, after World War II, the interdenominational Christian Democratic Union was formed and became one of the two major parties. However, religious issues have not thereby been fully eliminated from politics.

The loss of the predominantly Protestant areas in Prussia's Eastern provinces has meant that the Bundesrepublik is more Catholic than was pre-1945 Germany. According to the federal census of 1950,[64] the membership of the Roman Catholic Church amounted to 43.8 percent of the population. The largest Protestant body, the Evangelical Church, accounted for 51 percent.[65] The ratios in the individual Länder in 1950 show greater differences as indicated in the following table.

State	Evangelical population (percent)	Roman Catholic population (percent)
Schleswig-Holstein	88.0	6.0
Bremen	84.9	8.9
Hamburg	79.0	6.5
Lower Saxony	77.3	18.8
Hesse	64.3	32.2
Baden-Württemberg	50.7	47.2
North Rhine–Westphalia	41.1	54.8
Rhineland-Palatinate	40.8	57.7
Bavaria	26.8	71.9
The Saar	25.3	73.4

As a result of the tremendous influx of expellees and refugees, the religious complexion of municipalities, counties, and states was frequently altered. With the exception of Oldenburg, the territories which were united to form Lower Saxony were heavily Protestant. Now in that Land, a much larger percentage (18.8 percent) of the population is Catholic. On the other hand, the Protestants are stronger in North Rhine–Westphalia than they were before 1945: that strength has been increased since 1950 by refugee resettlement programs. Thus in 1957, 42.6 percent of the state's population was Evangelical and 52.5 percent was Catholic. The shifting of population has further complicated the already difficult problem of religion in the public schools.

With these facts in mind, it is easy to understand why the Catholic-Protestant *rapprochement* of the Hitler years has, since 1945, been weakened by the revival of religious issues in domestic politics. In part, this is due to the uncompromising policy of the Catholic Church, or at least of some elements within it.[66] There is thus posed a special difficulty for the Christian Democratic Union whose voting strength depends upon the maintenance of its interdenominational appeal. An important device in preserving CDU unity is the appropriate division of the political "loaves and fishes." One writer even speaks of "the rigid parity between Protestants and Catholics in filling offices at most levels from the Federal Government down to teaching posts in mixed schools."[67]

As for the Social Democratic Party, whatever its Marxist background may have been, it is no longer antireligious. It holds that, in a democracy, religion is an individual matter and that separation of church and state is desirable. To such doctrines, the Free Democratic Party also subscribes; it too has an anticlerical past but is not now antireligious. Indeed, there are many Protestants, both nominal and active, who vote for SPD or FDP tickets. But in campaigns, the CDU/CSU tends to emphasize the "Christian" character of its candidates and to paste opprobrious labels on their opponents.[68] Nevertheless, the examples just cited are not too significant.

Religion in the Public Schools

The really troublesome religious issue involves the public schools, especially the elementary schools (*Volksschulen*) with their eight or nine grades. In the United States, church and state are constitutionally separated and religion may not be taught in the public schools. This is in contrast to the Bundesrepublik where the basic question is, "How should the *Volksschulen* be organized with reference to religion?"[69] Should they be: (a) denominational or confessional schools (*Bekenntnisschulen*); (b) mixed or interdenominational Christian community schools (*Christliche Gemeinschaftsschulen, Christliche Simultanschulen*); or (c) secular community schools (*bekenntnisfreie Schulen*)?

The question is intimately connected with various guarantees contained in Articles 6 and 7 of the *Grundgesetz*. Parents have a "natural right" in the education of their children, including the right to decide about participation or nonparticipation of the children in religious instruction.[70] At the same time, religion is declared to be a regular subject of instruction in the public schools except for the secular schools.[71] In *Bekenntnisschulen,* all subjects are taught in the spirit of a particular religion. In other words, Catholic children are taught by Catholic teachers in Catholic public schools, and there are Evangelical schools and teachers for Evangelical children. In the *Christliche Gemeinschaftsschulen,* the children are separated by faiths only for religious instruction. However, in both types of schools, parents may ask to have their children excused from religious teaching and exercises, and teachers may not be compelled to teach religion against their wishes.

The great battle in the Bonn Constitutional Convention was not over the giving or not giving of religious instruction in the public schools but over the question of adopting the Weimar Constitution provision on traditional denominational schools. Article 146-2 of that document reads:[72]

> Within the *Gemeinden,* however, upon the request of those entitled to education, public elementary schools of their denomination or of their *Weltanschauung* are to be established insofar as this does not interfere with an organized school system in the sense of Paragraph 1 (of Article 146). As far as possible, the wishes of those entitled to education are to be considered. The details are to be fixed by state legislation in accordance with the fundamental principles of a Reich law.

This provision was not included in the *Grundgesetz* which merely refers to *Bekenntnisschulen* in a very indirect way (Article 7-5), thus leaving the question wholly to the Länder.

In 1931, over 83 percent of all elementary public schools in Germany were *Bekenntnisschulen.*[73] The Hitler regime, with its highly centralized control of education, changed the pattern. Notwithstanding the guarantees of the Reich-

Vatican Concordat of 1933, Nazi practice eventually abolished the organization of public schools along denominational lines.

At the end of World War II, with so many school buildings destroyed, necessity compelled the Western Allies to order the reopening of the schools on an interdenominational basis, but with final decision about denominational schools left to the German Land governments. They have dealt with it in different ways as is shown by the following statistics on *Volksschulen* in May 1953.[74]

Christliche Gemeinschaftsschulen	9,267
Gemeinschaftsschulen (only in Hamburg)	316
Evangelische Bekenntnisschulen	4,391
Katholische Bekenntnisschulen	10,806

The Catholic Church has been the strongest and most consistent supporter of *Bekenntnisschulen.* As early as 1946, the Conference of Bishops, meeting at Fulda, expressed itself vigorously on the subject, emphatically reaffirming Article 146 of the Weimar Constitution and Article 23 of the Concordat.[75] More recently, the Church has assailed the *Rahmenplan* of the German Committee for the Educational System because it does not give religion "a leading role in the educational function of the schools."[76]

Before 1933, the Evangelical Churches on the whole supported the *Bekenntnisschule.* This is still true of some *Landeskirchen,* particularly in Bavaria. On the other hand, many Evangelical Protestants now argue that the most important thing is adequate religious instruction. Where this is regularly and fully offered in the *Christliche Gemeinschaftsschule,* that type is best.[77] Mutual tolerance is thereby encouraged since children are not separated from each other at an early age because of religious differences. Moreover, the *Christliche Gemeinschaftsschule* can be larger and better equipped. The *Bekenntnisschule* places religious minorities at a disadvantage. Either the children must attend a school which is not of their denomination, or they must travel to a neighboring area which has such a school, or a small and poorer school of their own faith must be established for them.

It is not surprising that the *Bekenntnisschule* is the dominant pattern in the Saar and Bavaria where over 70 percent of the population is Catholic. Article 27 of the Saar Constitution flatly declares that the elementary public schools are *Bekenntnisschulen.* The Constitution of Bavaria (Article 135-1), at least in theory, sanctions alternatives. Nevertheless, the controversial elementary school law of 1950 heavily favored the confessional school. In 1952, of the *Volksschulen* in Bavaria, 5,104 were Catholic, 1,583 were Evangelical, and only 170 were *Gemeinschaftsschulen.*[78]

Catholics constitute a majority of the population in two other states, Rhineland-Palatinate and North Rhine–Westphalia. Article 29 of the Constitution of Rhineland-Palatinate is much like Article 135 of the Constitution of Bavaria. After eight years of "Schulkampf," the Landtag of Rhineland-Palatinate finally passed an elementary school bill in 1955.[79] Article 12 of the Constitution of North Rhine–Westphalia is somewhat more generous than what is offered in the Saar, Bavaria and Rhineland-Palatinate. Even so, there has also been conflict in that state.

Should elementary public school teachers be trained in denominational or interdenominational public teachers' colleges? This question was not specifically answered by the Constitution of Bavaria which merely states (Article 135-2) : "In the *Bekenntnisschulen,* only such teachers will be employed as are qualified and willing to instruct according to the principles of the faith concerned." For more than a decade, the problem was before the Landtag of Bavaria; it produced a cabinet upset; and it was not finally resolved by legislation until 1958.[80] The law now is that teachers' colleges must be of a denominational character but, if enough students want an interdenominational institution, it is to be created. The *Bekenntnis* teachers' college is also the rule in the Saar, Rhineland-Palatinate, North Rhine–Westphalia and Baden-Württemberg. In the other Länder, they are interdenominational except for the courses on religion.

While the *Bekenntnnisschule* is dominant in the Catholic Länder, it does not exist in Protestant Bremen, Hamburg, Hesse and Schleswig-Holstein. When Baden-Württemberg was formed, North and South Baden and North Württemberg had *Christliche Gemeinschaftsschulen;* but in Württemberg-Hohenzollern, both types of schools were authorized. In the Baden-Württemberg Constitution of 1953, the issue was compromised by Article 15 which maintains in the four parts of the Land the status quo as of December 1951.

The state in which the greatest battle took place was Lower Saxony and the occasion was the school law of 1954.[81] Although the population of that Land is predominantly Evangelical, the Catholics are strong in certain areas, such as the *Regierungsbezirk* of Osnabrück in which they number 51 percent of the people. Since Lower Saxony was a synthesis of three previously existing Länder and the Prussian province of Hanover, there was no common elementary school pattern before 1933. For example, Land Oldenburg had only *Bekenntnisschulen,* while Land Brunswick and Land Schaumburg-Lippe had *Gemeinschaftsschulen.* Because Oldenburg strongly objected to being swallowed up in Lower Saxony, a curious article (Article 55-2) was inserted in the Lower Saxon Constitution. The effect of this provision is to prevent Oldenburg's denominational school system from being changed except by constitutional amendment.[82] Because of this, Oldenburg was not involved in the dispute which mainly concerned the territories of the former Prussian province of Hanover.

A Prussian statute of 1906 had stipulated that, as a rule, in the elementary public schools, the instruction of Evangelical children should be by Evangelical teachers and that the same principle should hold for Catholic children.[83] Prior to 1933, this had caused no great difficulties in Hanover because, except for the large cities, the two confessions lived geographically separated from each other. However, the great influx of expellees and refugees after World War II produced a religiously mixed population so that only 10 percent of the *Volksschulen* were attended exclusively by children of one denomination. In about 40 percent of the schools, religious minorities ranged from 10 to 25 percent while in 171 other schools, the ratio was above 25 percent. Such was the situation when the school bill was introduced in the Landtag.

The act was sponsored by the SPD-BHE coalition cabinet with FDP support. It was strongly opposed by the Catholic Church and by some elements in the Evangelical Church. The law declared in favor of "fundamentally Christian schools" for all, with religious instruction given separately to Evangelical and Catholic children according to the principles of their respective faiths. However, upon the petition of parents and guardians, *Bekenntnisschulen* could be established under the following restrictions:

(a) Where there is only one *Volksschule* in the *Gemeinde*, it is to be for all denominations.[84]

(b) Where in a *Gemeinde* there are several small schools, below the prescribed standards, they are to be consolidated into a single school for all denominations.

(c) No *Bekenntnisschule* can be organized unless it will have 120 pupils; in *Gemeinden* of more than 5,000 inhabitants, there must be at least 240 pupils.

(d) A *Bekenntnisschule* cannot be organized unless there continues to be at least one *Gemeinschaftsschule* of appropriate size in the *Gemeinde*.

While the bill was under consideration, the Catholic bishops charged that it would be the death blow to most of the Catholic confessional schools. They appealed to the *Grundgesetz* and to Article 23 of the Concordat of 1933 which guarantees to the Catholic Church in Germany the right to have its *Bekenntnisschulen*. After the Landtag had enacted the measure, the Adenauer Cabinet took up the cudgels on behalf of the Church, stressing federal responsibilities under international treaties.

The champions of confessional schools had fought and lost the first round of the battle in the Bonn Constitutional Convention. They had not been able to secure the adoption of the Weimar Constitution provision on such schools (Article 146-2), nor had they been able to "anchor" the Concordat in the *Grundgesetz*.[85] Now they invoked the treaty power, always a difficult problem under federalism, as the struggle over the Bricker Amendment in the United States so well illustrates.

After long deliberation, the Federal Constitutional Court decided the case on March 26, 1957.[86] It disagreed with the Federal Cabinet and in effect upheld the authority of the Lower Saxony Landtag to enact the law. While in general the Federal Republic is the legal successor of the Reich with respect to treaty obligations, nevertheless, under the *Grundgesetz*, education is completely reserved to the states. Therefore, they have no legal obligation to the Bund to observe the school provisions of the Concordat. Thus a dangerous federal attack on the cultural autonomy of the Länder was foiled by the Court.

In spite of past struggles, the question of religion and the public schools, while important, should not be over-emphasized today. It does not arouse the average voter in the same way that the great debate over German rearmament did. But since it is a significant aspect of the perennial problem of the relation of church and state, it seems certain that it will continue to be one of the staples of politics in the Länder.

WEST GERMAN FEDERALISM TODAY

Twentieth-century federalism is not without its critics. It is alleged to be inefficient and wasteful, putting a premium on the irrational in finance, area and personnel. But over the years, federalism has proved itself to be an efficient device of constitutionalism, a check against arbitrary or excessive centralized rule. In the Bundesrepublik, such constitutionalism is especially necessary because of what the German nation and the world suffered from the National Socialist dictatorship.

In appraising the West German model, Americans should not assume that their own country has the sole pattern to be copied. Like other forms of government, successful federalism shows variations. The type established in the Bundesrepublik is very different from that in the United States, but this does not mean that it is inferior. As was noted earlier, the German variety is a "going concern," providing both unity and diversity, both stability and adaptability to peaceful change.

Admittedly, federalism is a relatively complex and sophisticated form of political organization. It cannot easily be set up overnight in a newly independent African state. Why, then, has it succeeded in West Germany which, fifteen years ago, seemed extremely unpromising?

Three reasons may be suggested. In the first place, the Federal Republic has been built upon the ancient German tradition of federalism, but without the aberrations caused by the special privileges of Prussia in the Bismarckian Reich. Prussia is no more, and the postwar Länder are sufficiently equal in area, population, and resources to be suitable "federal building blocks." Secondly, strong state governments were created between 1945 and 1949 before the federal superstructure was added. Finally, the balance of federal-state powers is maintained by effective control agencies such as the Bundesrat and the Federal Constitutional Court and by the way in which the party system has developed. Although the Bundesrepublik admittedly has shortcomings, it is, nevertheless, the best practicable state for the evolution of German constitutional democracy.

What are its prospects for the future?[87] The answer primarily depends upon what happens to a world full of revolutionary changes, torn by the rivalry of the Great Powers, and threatened with nuclear war. If peace can be maintained and tensions relaxed, there is every reason to believe that West German federal democracy will continue to build on the successful constitutional foundation and experiences of the past decade.

NOTES

NOTES FOR CHAPTER ONE

1. See Elmer Plischke, *Berlin: Development of Its Government and Administration*, published by the Historical Division, Office of the U.S. High Commissioner for Germany (Bad Godesberg, 1952); and Bruce L. R. Smith, "The Governance of Berlin," *International Conciliation*, No. 525 (November, 1959), pp. 171-230.

2. See Martin Drath, "Die staatsrechtliche Stellung Berlins," *Archiv des öffentlichen Rechts*, new series, vol. 43 (1957), pp. 27-75. On May 21, 1957, the Federal Constitutional Court handed down a decision dealing with the extent to which the West German Constitution applies to West Berlin. See *Entscheidungen des Bundesverfassungsgerichts* (hereafter cited as *BVerfGE.*), vol. 7 (Tübingen, 1958), pp. 1-17.

3. The financial assistance amounts to about one billion DM annually. In the decade 1948-1958, the U.S. Government contributed an additional 2.5 billion DM to West Berlin. See Joseph Wechsberg, "Letter from Berlin," *New Yorker*, vol. 34, No. 43 (December 13, 1958), pp. 158-189.

4. Area and population data are from the *Statistisches Jahrbuch für die Bundesrepublik Deutschland*, prepared by the Statistisches Bundesamt and published annually in Stuttgart. Maps showing state boundary lines are available in numerous sources. See, for example, Hans Kohn, *West Germany: New Era for German People*, Headline Series, Foreign Policy Association, No. 131 (New York, 1958), p. 11; Helmut Arntz, *Germany in a Nutshell*, published by the Press and Information Office of the Federal German Government (Wiesbaden, 1958), pp. 16-17; and Gwendolen M. Carter, John H. Herz and John C. Ranney, *Major Foreign Powers: The Governments of Great Britain, France, Germany and the Soviet Union* (3d ed., New York, 1957), p. 443.

5. The initial effect of establishing the four Allied zones of occupation in 1945 was to break up various existing territorial units. For details, see Edward H. Litchfield and Associates,

Governing Postwar Germany (Ithaca, 1953), pp. 87-92. On the pre-1945 territorial units, see James K. Pollock and Homer Thomas, *Germany in Power and Eclipse* (New York, 1952).

6. Laing Gray Cowan, *France and the Saar, 1680-1948* (New York, 1950); Frank M. Russell, *The Saar: Battleground and Pawn* (Stanford, California, 1951); Ludwig Dischler, *Das Saarland* (2 vols., Hamburg, 1956); and Jacques Freymond, *The Saar Conflict, 1945-1955* (London, 1960).

7. For the texts of the agreements of October 27, 1956, see *Bundesgesetzblatt*, 1956, vol. 2, pp. 1587-1876. References to the *Bundesgesetzblatt* are hereafter cited *BGBl*.

8. J. F. J. Gillen, *State and Local Government in West Germany, 1945-1953*, Historical Division, Office of the U.S. High Commissioner for Germany (Bad Godesberg, 1953), pp. 43-47.

9. For the text of the Constitution and also of the state constitutions, see Rudolf Werner Füsslein, ed., *Deutsche Verfassungen. Grundgesetz und deutsche Landesverfassungen* (3d ed., Berlin, 1959).

10. There was an advisory referendum on September 24, 1950 which had yielded similar results. Richard Schachtner, *Die deutschen Nachkriegswahlen* (Munich, 1956), p. 23.

11. *BGBl.*, 1951, I, pp. 283-287.

12. *BVerfGE.*, vol. 1 (1952), pp. 14-66. See also Gerhard Leibholz, "The Federal Constitutional Court and the 'Southwest Case,'" *American Political Science Review*, vol. 46 (1952), pp. 723-731; and Friedrich Klein, "Bundesverfassungsgericht und Südweststaatsfrage," *Archiv des öffentlichen Rechts*, new series, vol. 38 (1951-1952), pp. 452-464.

13. *BGBl.*, 1955, I, pp. 835-840.

14. *BVerfGE.*, vol. 5 (1956), pp. 34-56. See also Friedrich Klien, "Bundesverfassungsgericht und Altbadenfrage. Grundsätzliches zur Neugliederung des Bundesgebietes," *Archiv des öffentlichen Rechts*, new series, vol. 43 (1957), pp. 327-350.

15. Theodor Eschenburg, *Staat und Gesellschaft in Deutschland* (2d ed., Stuttgart, 1957), p. 366.

16. *Die Zeit*, March 28, 1957; *Frankfurter Allgemeine Zeitung* (Frankfurt), January 24, 1959.

17. *Stuttgarter Zeitung* (Stuttgart), July 3, 1957.

18. Eschenburg, *op. cit.*, pp. 365-366.

19. "Sizilianisches aus Baden," *Rheinischer Merkur* (Cologne), June 26 and July 3, 1959; *Die Zeit*, May 27, 1960.

20. Litchfield, *op. cit.*, p. 577.

21. *Die Neugliederung des Bundesgebiets. Gutachten des von der Bundesregierung eingesetzten Sachverständigenausschusses,* published by the Federal Ministry of the Interior (Bonn, 1955).

22. *BGBl.*, 1955, I, pp. 835-840.

23. Initiative petitions were requested in certain other areas in 1956 when the Volksbegehren took place in Lower Saxony and Rhineland-Palatinate. Thus the cities of Lübeck and Geesthacht wanted to transfer from Schleswig-Holstein to Hamburg, and 65 South Hessian Gemeinden wished to join Baden-Württemberg. The Federal Constitutional Court upheld the denial of these requests by the Federal Minister of the Interior, ruling that Article 29-2 referred only to territorial changes made by the occupying powers. See *BVerfGE.*, vol. 5 (1956), pp. 56-70; *ibid.*, vol. 6 (1957), pp. 20-32.

24. Schachtner, *op. cit., passim.*

25. Heinrich David, "Landkarten-Korrektur: Erst nach dem 'Tage X,' " *Die Zeit*, December 10, 1957.

26. There are also various American states which contain "depressed areas" suffering from the decline or loss of key industries.

27. Department of Commerce statistics as reported in the *New York Times*, August 15, 1960.

28. "Das Sozialprodukt der Länder der Bundesrepublik 1950 bis 1955," *Wirtschaft und Statistik,* published monthly by the Statistisches Bundesamt, new series, vol. 9 (Stuttgart, 1957), pp. 595-600.

29. Leo W. Schwartz, *Refugees in Germany Today: Their Legal Status and Integration* (New York, 1957); and Eugen Lemberg and others, *Die Vertriebenen in West Deutschland* (3 vols., Kiel, 1959). On the origins of the expellee-refugee problem, see Elizabeth Wiskemann, *Germany's Eastern Neighbors: Problems Relating to the Oder-Neisse Line and the Czech Frontier Region* (London, 1953).

30. Bureau of the Census, *Historical Statistics of the United States, 1789-1945* (Washington, D.C., 1949) pp. 33-34.

31. In 1958, there were about 12,475,000 of these people living in West Germany, of whom 2,188,000 had fled from Communist East Germany between September 1949 and December 1958. Federal Ministry for Expellees, Refugees and War Victims, *Facts concerning the Problem of German Expellees*

116   THE STATES IN WEST GERMAN FEDERALISM

and Refugees (5th ed., Bonn, 1960), *passim*. Since then, the flow has continued, rising sharply as a result of the collectivization measures in the spring of 1960 which were directed against farmers, craftsmen and small businessmen.

32. For the text as revised in 1957, see *BGBl.*, 1957, I, pp. 1215-1238. For the text of the Lastenausgleichgesetz or Equalization of Burdens Law, see *BGBl.*, 1952, I, pp. 446 ff. The latter statute established an equalization of burdens scheme, financed by a capital levy, to help refugees and other persons who had suffered war damage. Between 1949 and 1958, West German governments, federal, state and local, spent over 42 billion DM on refugee aid, housing, resettlement and employment. The expenditure has paid off; the refugees have greatly strengthened the German labor force and have thus aided reconstruction.

33. *Frankfurter Allgemeine Zeitung,* April 19, 1959.

34. To say nothing of almost 1,500 estates, mostly held by imperial knights (Reichsritter). Arnold Brecht, *Federalism and Regionalism in Germany: the Division of Prussia* (New York, 1945), pp. 7-8.

35. The National Socialists talked much about Reichsreform but did little. See Walter Baum, "Die 'Reichsreform' im Dritten Reich," *Vierteljahresheft für Zeitgeschichte,* vol. 3 (1955), pp. 36-56. Reichsreform had been much discussed before Hitler came to power in 1933. See Brecht, *op. cit.;* and Robert E. Dickinson, *The Regions of Germany,* (New York, 1945).

NOTES FOR CHAPTER TWO

1. The Schleswig-Holstein Constitution of 1949 is called a "Landessatzung." On the provisional constitutions which preceded the permanent constitutions, see Edward H. Litchfield and Associates, *Governing Postwar Germany* (Ithaca, 1953), pp. 101-102. For the texts of the state constitutions see Rudolf Werner Füsslein, ed., *Deutsche Verfassungen. Grundgesetz und deutsche Landesverfassungen* (3d ed., Berlin, 1959). Detailed studies of most of the state constitutions have been published in the *Jahrbuch des öffentlichen Rechts der Gegenwart,* edited by Gerhard Leibholz, new series, vols. 3, 5, 6, 7 (Tübingen, 1954-1958).

2. In Bavaria and North Rhine–Westphalia, the electorate

voted on the constitution as a whole. In the other three states, there was also a separate vote on a particular article: Hesse, Article 41 on socialization; Bremen, Article 47 on labor's right of codetermination (Mitbestimmungsrecht); and Rhineland-Palatinate, Article 29 on confessional public schools (Bekenntnisschulen).

3. Litchfield, *op. cit.*, note 66, pp. 104-105; and Füsslein, *op. cit., passim.*

4. In the German Land constitutions, most articles are short, having only one, two or three sentences.

5. *The Book of the States,* published by the Council of State Governments, 1954-1955, vol. 10 (Chicago, 1954), pp. 68-73. Only eight American states have constitutions shorter than Bavaria has.

6. Constitution of Baden-Württemberg, Article 2; Constitution of North Rhine–Westphalia, Article 4.

7. For the texts of the federal and state constitutions of the Weimar period, see Otto Ruthenberg, ed., *Verfassungsgesetze des Deutschen Reichs und der deutschen Länder* (Berlin, 1926).

8. George Stambuk, "Judicial Protection of Civil Liberties in Germany," *Political Studies,* vol. 4 (1956), pp. 190-194. All the Länder (except Schleswig-Holstein which uses the Federal Constitutional Court for cases arising under the state constitution) have state constitutional courts (Landesverfassungsgerichte). See Otto Bacholf and Dietrich Jesch, "Die Rechtsprechung der Landesverfassungsgerichte in der Bundesrepublik Deutschland." *Jahrbuch des öffentlichen Rechts der Gegenwart,* new series, vol. 6 (Tübingen, 1957), pp. 47-108.

9. On freedom of speech, see Frede Castberg, *Freedom of Speech in the West: A Comparative Study of Public Law in France, the United States and Germany* (New York, 1960).

10. For a different view, see Carl J. Friedrich in Arnold J. Zurcher, ed., *Constitutions and Constitutional Trends since World War II* (2d ed., New York, 1955), p. 28. Friedrich writes that the West German state constitutions, notably Bavaria (Article 48) and North Rhine–Westphalia (Article 60), "contain rather inadequate emergency provisions."

11. For an extensive bibliography on parties and elections, see John Brown Mason, "Government, Administration and Politics in West Germany: A Selected Bibliography," *American Political Science Review,* vol. 52 (1958), pp. 513-530. Particular

reference should be made to Arnold J. Heidenheimer, "Federalism and the Party System: The Case of West Germany," *American Political Science Review,* vol. 52 (1958), pp. 809-828; and Ossip K. Flechtheim, "Bund und Länder in der Sicht der Parteien," *Zeitschrift für Politik,* new series, vol. 4 (1957), pp. 348-361.

12. For a discussion of this article, see Carl J. Schneider, "Political Parties and the German Basic Law of 1949," *Western Political Quarterly,* vol. 10 (1957), pp. 527-540.

13. "SPD" stands for Sozialdemokratische Partei Deutschlands; "CDU" for Christlich-Demokratische Union. The Bavarian affiliate of the CDU is the Christian Social Union (CSU).

14. Norbert Muhlen, *A Report of Germany before the Elections,* published by the American Council on Germany just prior to the Bundestag election of 1957 (New York, 1957), p. 4.

15. The Refugee Party was first called the "Bloc of Expellees and Victims of Injustice" (Block der Heimatvertriebenen und Entrechteten, which was abbreviated to "BHE"). Later it took the name "All-German Bloc" (Gesamtdeutscher Block or GB). The two abbreviations are now usually written together, GB-BHE.

16. *New York Times,* July 2, 1960.

17. *BVerfGE.,* vol. 2 (1953), pp. 1-79.

18. In the Rhineland-Palatinate Landtag election of April 26, 1959, the Deutsche Reichspartei polled 5.1 percent of the popular vote. *New York Times,* May 3, 1959.

19. *BVerfGE.,* vol. 5 (1956), pp. 85-393. See Edward McWhinney, "The German Federal Constitutional Court and the Communist Party Decision," *Indiana Law Journal,* vol. 32 (1957), pp. 295-310.

20. See "Kennwort 'Sendepause,'" *Die Zeit,* December 18, 1959.

21. Eschenburg says that Landtag elections can in effect operate as federal by-elections (Nachwahlen). Theodor Eschenburg, *Staat und Gesellschaft in Deutschland* (2d ed., Stuttgart, 1957), p. 628.

22. For a full analysis of this problem, see Heidenheimer, "Federalism and the Party System," *op. cit.*

23. For a spirited defense of state politics and politicians, see "Die Oekonomie von Bund und Ländern," *Deutsche Rundschau,* vol. 84 (1958), pp. 609-610.

24. For criticism of German proposals to hold all elections on the same day, see Theodor Eschenburg, *Die Zeit,* June 19, 1958.

25. *New York Times,* November 10 and 11, 1957.

26. Richard Schachtner, *Die deutschen Nachkriegswahlen* (Munich, 1956), *passim.* Statistics on Landtag elections are also given in the *Statistisches Jahrbuch für die Bundesrepublik Deutschland.* The West Berliners have consistently had the best voting records; in the West Berlin state legislature election of December 7, 1958, 93.7 percent of the registered electors voted.

27. According to Rupert Breitling, "Die Wählerschaft modelliert am Parteisystem. Die Wahlergebnisse in Bund und Ländern seit 1945," *Die Gegenwart,* vol. 12 (1957), pp. 332-336. For a further comment, on this point and on other political activities of women, see Gabriele Bremme, *Die politische Rolle der Frau in Deutschland* (Göttingen, 1956); and Henry P. Pilgert, *Women in West Germany,* Historical Division, Office of the U.S. High Commissioner for Germany (Bad Godesberg, 1952).

28. For details on the SPD and CDU, see Alfred Grosser, "Rapport sur la structure du Parti social-democrate d'Allemagne (S.P.D.)," *Occidente,* vol. 11 (Turin, Italy, 1955), pp. 56-83; Arno Scholz and Walter Oschelwoski, eds., *Aufgabe und Leistung der deutschen Sozialdemokratie in Ländern und Gemeinden* (Berlin, 1956); Gerhard Schulz, "Die Organisationsstruktur der CDU," *Zeitschrift für Politik,* new series, vol. 3 (1956), pp. 147-165; and Arnold J. Heidenheimer, "La structure confessionelle, sociale et régionale de la CDU," *Revue française de science politique,* vol. 7 (1957), pp. 626-645.

29. See Arthur W. Macmahon, ed., *Federalism, Mature and Emergent* (Garden City, New York, 1955), chaps. 7 and 8. It may be conceded that the checks are more important in the United States than in West Germany where there are complaints about party centralization. Critics assert that the CDU under Adenauer has become a *"Kanzlerpartei."* However, it is by no means certain that this kind of centralization can be maintained after Adenauer leaves office.

30. Walter Dirks "Ein Grunsatzprogramm. Zum 'neuen Weg' der Sozialdemokratischen Partei Deutschlands," *Frankfurter Hefte,* vol. 15 (1960), pp. 1-5; and Lewis J. Edinger and Douglas A. Chalmers, "Overture or Swan Song: German Social Democracy Prepares for a New Decade," *Antioch Review,* vol. 20 (1960), pp. 163-175.

31. In June 1959, the Federal Ministry of the Interior sent a draft of a party law to the Bundesrat. This bill provoked a lively but inconclusive debate in the Bundestag in February 1960. See Ludwig Bergsträsser, "Der Entwurf des Parteigesetzes," *Politische Studien,* vol. 10 (1959), pp. 596-605; and Theodor Eschenburg's discussion in *Die Zeit,* February 23, 1960.

32. W. Grundmann, "Die Finanzierung der politischen Parteien," *Zeitschrift für die gesamte Staatswissenschaft,* vol. 115 (1959), pp. 113-130; Arnold J. Heidenheimer, "German Party Finance: the CDU," *American Political Science Review,* vol. 51 (1957), pp. 369-385; and G. Triesch, "Die Finanzierung der SPD," *Politische Meinung,* vol. 3 (1958), pp. 36-51. See also *BVerfGE.,* vol. 8 (1959), pp. 51-71.

33. Otto Kirchheimer, "The Political Scene in West Germany," *World Politics,* vol. 9 (1957), pp. 433-445, at p. 439. Although they are frequently referred to in the pages of the present work, this study does not include a separate discussion of organized groups other than political parties. See Mason's bibliography, *op. cit.*

34. For details about state and federal election legislation, see Klaus Otto Nass, *Wahlorgane und Wahlerfahren bei Bundestag- und Landtagswahlen* (Göttingen, 1959).

35. Schachtner, *op. cit.,* pp. 79-94; and Dolf Sternberger, "Bildung und Formen der Koalitionsregierung," *Zeitschrift für Politik,* new series, vol. 1 (1954), pp. 47-70.

36. After his great victory in the 1957 Bundestag election, Adenauer could have formed a one-party CDU cabinet but did not do so.

37. On the complexity of politics in Lower Saxony, see Walther and Guenther Schuetze's chapter, "La Basse-Saxe," in Alfred Grosser, ed., *Administration et Politique en Allemagne occidentale* (Paris, 1954). For a detailed study of the struggle over the formation of the Lower Saxon cabinet in 1951, see Götz Roth, *Fraktion und Regierung* (Meisenheim am Glan, 1954).

38. Hesse, Gemeindeordnung, Article 80, *Gesetz- und Verordnungsblatt (GVBl.),* 1952, p. 11.

39. Klaus Altmeyer, "Die Volksbefragung an der Saar vom 23. Oktober 1955," *Europa-Archiv,* vol. 11 (1956), pp. 9049-9060.

40. Bavaria, Gemeindeordnung, Article 11, *GVBl.,* 1952, p. 19. For the referendum in Landkreis Friedberg, Bavaria (1950),

see *Neue Zeitung* (Frankfurt), April 4, 1950. For the referendum in the Württemberg Gemeinde of Bad Wimpfen (1951), see *ibid.,* May 7, 1952.

41. For a discussion of public opinion polls, see W. Phillips Davison, "Trends in West German Public Opinion, 1946-1956," in Speier and Davison, *op. cit.,* chap. 8; and Gerhard Schmidtchen, *Die befragte Nation* (Heidelberg, 1959).

42. Elisabeth B. Noelle and Erich Peter Naumann, eds., *Jahrbuch der öffentlichen Meinung, 1947-1955* (Allensbach, 1956), pp. 278-308; and *Jahrbuch der öffentlichen Meinung, 1956* (Allensbach, 1957), pp. 280-295.

43. Allen C. Siebens, "Europa Union Plebiscites," *Information Bulletin,* published monthly by the Office of the U.S. High Commissioner for Germany, September 1950, pp. 15-17, 23.

44. *Die Gegenwart,* vol. 6, No. 9 (May 1, 1951), pp. 1-6.

45. On the rearmament debate in general, see Gordon A. Craig, "Germany and NATO. The Rearmament Debate, 1950-1958," in Klaus Knorr, ed., *NATO and American Security* (Princeton, 1959), chap. 10. See also Gerard Braunthal, "Direct and Representative Democracy in West Germany: The Atomic Armament Issue," *Canadian Journal of Economics and Political Science,* vol. 25 (1959), pp. 313-323.

46. Bremen, *GVBl.,* 1958, p. 49; Hamburg, *GVBl.,* 1958, p. 141.

47. *BVerfGE.,* vol. 8 (1959), pp. 104-122. See also Ernst-Werner Fuss, "Die Nichtigerklärung der Volksbefragungsgesetze von Hamburg und Bremen," *Archiv des öffentlichen Rechts,* new series, vol. 44 (1958), pp. 383-422; and Theodor Maunz, "Grundgesetz und Volksbefragungsgesetze," *Die öffentliche Verwaltung,* vol. 12 (1959), pp. 1-5.

48. *BVerfGE.,* vol. 8 (1959), pp. 122-141.

49. The Weimar Constitution of 1919 was even more specific. By Article 17 of that document, the parliamentary form of government was required in each state, and state and local representative bodies had to be chosen "according to the fundamental principles of proportional representation."

50. For detailed information on the state governments, see A. Koehler and K. Jansen, eds., *Die Bundesrepublik, 1958/59* (Berlin, 1958). For an excellent brief account, see Richard Hiscocks, *Democracy in Western Germany* (London, 1957), chap. 7, "Government in the Länder." On the developments of state

cabinets and legislatures in the early postwar years, see Litchfield, op. cit., pp. 94-109.

51. With the possible exception of Bavaria. However, in
practice, Bavaria has the parliamentary form of government.
Eschenburg has argued against the suitability of the parlia-
mentary form for the state governments. Theodor Eschenburg,
"Das Regierungssystem unserer Länder ist falsch," Die Zeit,
July 8, 1960.

52. In Bremen and Hamburg, the Landesregierung has the
traditional name of "Senat." All the senators are elected by the
legislature (Bürgerschaft). Instead of a minister-president, there
is a "Bürgermeister und Senatspräsident" in Bremen, and an
"Erster Bürgermeister" in Hamburg. Each is elected by the
senators from among their own number. A peculiarity of the
Bremen Constitution (Article 108) is that senators may not
simultaneously be members of the Bürgerschaft, although they
continue to have full access to that body as senators. A Bürgerschaft member who is elected senator must, therefore, resign
his legislative seat.

53. New York Times, February 21, 1956; and Heidenheimer,
"Federalism and the Party System: The Case of West Germany,"
op. cit., passim.

54. Hanns Seidel (CSU) thereupon formed a new coalition
cabinet (CSU-FDP-GB/BHE) from which the SPD was excluded.
Die Zeit, October 17, 1957.

55. New York Times, September 6, 1950. For details as to the
personnel and terms of office of all state cabinets, 1945-1956,
see Schachtner, op. cit., pp. 79-94.

56. On the Schlueter case, see Thomas T. Helde, "Academic
Freedom and German Politics: The Göttingen Incident," Yale
Review, vol. 47 (1957-1958), pp. 77-92.

57. Theodor Eschenburg, "Wie kann ein Minister entlassen
werden? Erst Schlueter und darauf Asbach," Die Zeit, January
2, 1958. In connection with the scandals of the Auerbach case,
the Bavarian Minister of Justice, Dr. Josef Müller, was forced
to resign (1952). Neue Zeitung, August 15, 1952. The Bavarian
lottery scandal resulted in prison sentences (1959) for former
Deputy Minister President Josef Baumgartner, chairman of the
Bavarian Party, and for former Minister of the Interior, August
Geislhöringer (BP); on appeal, new trials were ordered. Rheinischer Merkur, August 14, 1959 and February 26, 1960.

NOTES
58. "Minister werden ist sehr schwer; Minister bleiben nicht
so sehr." Quoted from *Die Zeit,* August 29, 1957. This was
Long under heavy fire because of his connections with the
Nazi regime, he was finally forced to resign. He did so on May
3, 1960, two days after his 55th birthday when he became eligible
to retire on a minister's pension. *New York Times,* April 9 and
May 4, 1960.
59. On Landtag membership and rules of procedure, see
W. Burhenne, ed., *Recht und Organisation der Parlamente*
(Bielefeld, 1958).
60. On the Bavarian Senate, see Taylor Cole, "Functional
Representation in the German Federal Republic," *Midwest
Journal of Political Science,* vol. 2 (1958), pp. 256-277. The
61. Bavaria had only 7 women deputies (3.4 percent) but
Bremen had 13. Gabriele Bremme, *Die politische Rolle der
Frau in Deutschland, op. cit.,* p. 136.
62. *New York Times,* September 20, 1959.
63. See Gwendolen M. Carter, John H. Herz and John C.
Ranney, *Major Foreign Powers. The Governments of Great
Britain, France, Germany and the Soviet Union* (3d ed., New
York, 1957), pp. 465-467.
64. From the data given in the *Amtliches Handbuch des
Deutschen Bundestages, 3. Wahlperiode* (Darmstadt, 1958), the
writer counted 167 out of 519 members who were in this
65. Otto Kirchheimer, "The Political Scene in West Ger-
66. There was also some German support for the British and
American arguments. See Theodor Eschenburg, *Der Beamte
67. Litchfield, *op. cit.,* p. 291.
68. *Stuttgarter Zeitung,* July 2, 1957.
69. Theodor Eschenburg, "Ämterpatronage im Parteienstaat,"
Politische Studien, vol. 5 (1955), pp. 23-27.
70. Carter, Herz and Ranney, *op. cit.,* p. 466.
71. See Theodor Eschenburg, "Abgeordnete zwischen zwei
Pflichten. Politik und Geschäft—wie können sie auseinander

72. In both the United States and West Germany, the compensation of state legislators compares unfavorably with that received by members of Congress and the Bundestag. In Schleswig-Holstein, the monthly compensation of the deputies is 300 DM to which is added a per diem of 25 DM for each daily session of the legislature or committee meeting which is attended. *GVBl.*, 1955, p. 125. It is customary to pay more to certain officials of the Landtag. Thus in Schleswig-Holstein, the Landtag President receives 800 DM monthly and the Leader of the Opposition (a unique provision) 600 DM monthly.

73. Theodor Eschenburg, "Sichert die Abgeordneten! Verantwortung wird schlecht bezahlt," *Die Zeit*, November 21, 1957.

74. *Ibid.*, June 6, 1950.

75. Gesetzblatt *(GBL.)* or Gesetz- und Verordnungsblatt *(GVBl.)*.

76. Between 1954 and 1956, the Landtag of Hesse passed 22 laws; from 1955 to 1957, the Landtag of Rhineland-Palatinate passed 30 laws. Peter H. Merkl, "Executive-Legislative Federalism in West Germany," *American Political Science Review*, vol. 53 (1959), pp. 732-741, at p. 734.

77. There have also been extensive codifications of state law. See *Bereinigte Sammlung des bayerischen Landesrechts, 1802-1956* (5 vols., Munich, 1957); and *Sammlung des bereinigten niedersächsischen Landesrechts, 1945-1958* (Hanover, 1960).

78. Heinrich Korte in *Jahrbuch des öffentlichen Rechts der Gegenwart*, new series, vol. 5 (Tübingen, 1956), p. 147.

79. In each state, the Rechnungshof is an independent body responsible only to the Landtag. See Richard Tüngle, "Kontrolle der Behörden. Die Rechnungshöfe ermöglichen Kritik durch die Parlamente," *Die Zeit*, June 17, 1954.

80. Eschenburg, *Staat und Gesellschaft in Deutschland, op. cit.*, p. 590.

81. Hiscocks notes that the Landtag proceedings are less formal than those of the Bundestag. Hiscocks, *op. cit.*, p. 160.

82. On these topics, see the studies edited by Dolf Strenberger and entitled, *Parteien, Regierungen, Fraktionen* (8 vols., Meisenheim am Glan, 1954-1956). Most of these are listed in Mason's bibliography, *op. cit.*

83. See Klemens Kramer, *Der Abgeordnete zwischen Entscheidungsfreiheit und Parteidiziplin* (Munich, 1953; 2d ed., 1958).

84. In some states, two readings are prescribed; in others, three.

85. *Neue Zeitung,* March 26, 1953.

86. *Die Gegenwart,* vol. 10 (1955), pp. 848-849; *Rheinischer Merkur,* August 14, 1959; February 26, 1960.

87. Heinrich Korte in *Jahrbuch des öffentlichen Rechts der Gegenwart,* vol. 5, *op. cit.,* pp. 72-73.

NOTES FOR CHAPTER THREE

1. For a detailed account, which also contains an extensive bibliography, see John Ford Golay, *The Founding of the Federal Republic of Germany* (Chicago, 1958).

2. See Ossip K. Flechtheim, ed., *Bund und Länder* (Berlin, 1959).

3. On the subject matter of this chapter, see Gottfried Dietze, "The Federal Republic of Germany: An Evaluation after Ten Years," *Journal of Politics,* vol. 22 (1960), pp. 112-147; Arnold J. Heidenheimer, "Federalism and the Party System: The Case of West Germany," *American Political Science Review,* vol. 52 (1958), pp. 809-828; Peter H. Merkl, "Executive-Legislative Federalism in West Germany," *ibid.,* vol. 53 (1959), pp. 732-741; Karlheinz Neunreither, "Politics and Bureaucracy in the West German Bundesrat," *ibid.,* vol. 53 (1959), pp. 713-731 and, by the same author, "Federalism and West German Bureaucracy," *Political Studies,* vol. 7 (1959), pp. 233-245. See also Karlheinz Neunreither, *Der Bundesrat zwischen Politik und Verwaltung* (Heidelberg, 1959).

4. For details on the composition, procedure and powers of the Bundesrat, see Hans Schäfer, *Der Bundesrat* (Cologne, 1955); and the official *Handbuch des Bundesrates* (Darmstadt, 1958).

5. Taylor Cole, "The West German Constitutional Court: An Appraisal after Six Years," *Journal of Politics,* vol. 20 (1958), pp. 278-307; "Three Constitutional Courts," *American Political Science Review,* vol. 53 (1959), pp. 963-984; and "The Bundesverfassungsgericht, 1956-1958. An American Appraisal," *Jahrbuch des öffentlichen Rechts der Gegenwart,* new series, vol. 8 (Tübingen, 1959), pp. 29-47.

6. The conflict has been acute in questions relating to foreign

policy and defense, particularly when constitutional amendments were necessary. The Bundesrat may appeal to the Federal Constitutional Court.

7. August Dresbach, "Das Parlament der Ministerialbeamten," *Frankfurter Allgemeine Zeitung*, May 23, 1957.

8. Bundesministerium für Angelegenheiten des Bundesrates und der Länder.

9. For a pen picture of von Merkatz, see Christoph Quint, "Ein Föderalist aus Pommern," *Rheinischer Merkur*, May 1, 1959.

10. See Karlheinz Neunreither, *op. cit.*; and Peter M. Merkl, *op. cit.*

11. See Karl Loewenstein in Edward H. Litchfield and Associates, *Governing Postwar Germany* (Ithaca, 1953), chap. 9; and Gwendolen M. Carter, John H. Herz and John C. Ranney, *Major Foreign Powers: The Governments of Great Britain, France, Germany and the Soviet Union* (3d ed., New York, 1957), chap. 6.

12. *BGBl.*, 1959, I, pp. 745-755. See also Otto-Ernst Starke, "Das Gesetz über die Deutsche Bundesbank und seine wichtigsten öffentlichen-rechtlichen Probleme," *Die öffentliche Verwaltung*, vol. 10 (1957), pp. 606-612.

13. On the Bank deutscher Länder, see Litchfield, *op. cit.*, pp. 427-434.

14. However, a cabinet bill on the regulation of credit (Kreditwesengesetz) met strong opposition in the Bundesrat because it proposed to use federal rather than state administrative agencies. See "Länder gegen zentrale Bankaufsicht," *Frankfurter Allgemeine Zeitung*, March 21, 1959.

15. *Ibid.*, May 5, 1959.

16. In West Germany, state and local agencies are used in Bundestag elections but federal laws and ordinances cover most of the details. The election administrative hierarchy is headed by the Federal Election Commissioner (Bundeswahlleiter) who is appointed by the Federal Minister of the Interior. See Bundeswahlgesetz, May 7, 1956, *BGBl.*, 1956, I, pp. 383-407; and James K. Pollock and others, *German Democracy at Work* (Ann Arbor, 1955), chap. 5.

17. Neunreither, "Politics and Bureaucracy in the West German Bundesrat," *op. cit.*, p. 713.

18. Theodor Eschenburg, *Staat und Gesellschaft in Deutsch-*

land (2d ed., Stuttgart, 1957), pp. 763-765. See also Hans Schäfer, "Die bundeseigene Verwaltung," *Die öffentliche Verwaltung,* vol. 11 (1958), pp. 241-248. For details on landeseigene Verwaltung, see Article 84 of the Grundgesetz. Chapter VIII of that document (Article 83-91) deals with the execution of federal laws in general.

19. "Personal des Bundes, der Länder und Gemeinden am 2. Oktober 1955," Statistisches Bundesamt, *Wirtschaft und Statistik,* new series, vol. 8 (1956), pp. 464-467.

20. According to Dr. Franz Meyers, Minister-President of North Rhine–Westphalia, as reported in the *New York Times,* November 8, 1959.

21. In 1959, there were 94,674 officials, employees and workers in the direct service of the state of Lower Saxony. *Die Zeit,* December 11, 1959.

22. For American examples, see the reports of the Commission on Intergovernmental Relations (16 vols., Washington, D.C., 1955).

23. On the joint machinery for appointments to federal judicial bodies, see Articles 95 and 96 of the Grundgesetz. The federal and state legislators have an organization with headquarters at Bonn which is called the "Interparlamentarische Arbeitsgemeinschaft." It publishes a weekly periodical, *Parlamentsspiegel* and sponsored the volume compiled by W. Burhenne and entitled, *Recht und Organisation der Parlamente* (Bielefeld, 1958).

24. *BGBl.,* 1951, I, pp. 165-166.; *BGBl.,* 1950, I, p. 682.

25. The Conference of Land Ministers-President, meeting at Munich in February 1954, criticized the Bundesamt für Verfassungsschutz. See "Von der Länderkonferenz," *Die Gegenwart,* vol. 9 (1954), pp. 101-102.

26. These are largely an inheritance from the Nazi Reich and the former state of Prussia. As recently as 1957, the West German Federal Government and the Länder owned or controlled about 25 percent of the nation's heavy industry. *New York Times,* February 3, 1957.

27. The Federal Government is now engaged in a program of reducing its holdings through the sale of company securities to small private investors. *New York Times,* February 22, 1959. Under federal legislation passed in 1960, the Volkswagen works is being transferred to private ownership but with the Bund and

Lower Saxony each retaining 20 percent of the shares. See *BGBl.*, 1960, I, pp. 301-302 and 585-587.

28. See *Der Städtetag*, new series, vol. 11 (1958), p. 309.

29. For a discussion of these laws, see Hans Schneider, "Körperschaftliche Verbundverwaltung. Verfassungsrechtliche Betrachtungen über die Bildung von landesunmittelbaren und bundesunmittelbaren Verwaltungsträger durch Bundesgesetz," *Archiv des öffentlichen Rechts*, new series, vol. 44 (1958), pp. 1-25.

30. Such as social insurance, health and welfare. See Hertha Kraus in Litchfield, *op. cit.*, chap. 15.

31. *Wirtschaft und Statistik*, new series, vol. 12 (1960), pp. 170-172; and *New York Times*, January 13, 1959. See also Robert G. Wertheimer, "The Miracle of German Housing in the Postwar Period," *Land Economics*, vol. 34 (1958), pp. 338-345; and Hermann Wanderslob, ed., *Handwörterbuch des Städtebaues, Wohnungs- und Siedlungswesens* (3 vols., Stuttgart, 1955-1959). Although most of the money was from German sources, the United States also contributed. From the beginning of the Marshall Plan through 1954, American aid for all types of German housing amounted to 750,000,000 DM. *Department of State Bulletin*, vol. 32 (1955), p. 189.

32. *BGBl.*, 1950, I, pp. 83-88, as amended *ibid.*, 1953, I, pp. 1037-1046. Second Housing Act, *ibid.*, 1956, I, pp. 523-558. An examination of the *Bundesgesetzblatt* from 1949 to date discloses additional statutes affecting housing. The most recent of these is the law of 1960 which, among other things, is designed to reduce and eventually eliminate housing and rent controls on older dwellings, that is, on those built before June 20, 1948. See *BGBl.*, 1960, I, pp. 389-426.

33. On the organization of the Federal Ministry of Housing and of the state housing agencies, see A. Koehler and K. Jansen, eds., *Die Bundesrepublik, 1958/59* (Berlin, 1958), *passim*.

34. Twenty-five percent from 1955 to 1958. For a discussion of this and other forms of government assistance, see "The Solution of the Housing Problem in the Federal Republic of Germany," *International Labour Review*, vol. 72 (1955), pp. 187-202.

35. Ten percent of the building cost in each of the first two years and 3 percent in each of the subsequent ten years. These percentages were reduced in 1960. See Arthur J. Olsen, "Bonn

Curbs Boom by Tax Increases," *New York Times,* March 10, 1960.

36. Wage earners may receive government premiums for savings toward home building. The premium amounts to 25 percent of the payments made to a building and loan association (Bausparkasse) for the purpose of obtaining a loan or for the purchase of shares in a housing cooperative. The premium is paid directly to the institution concerned but may not exceed 400 DM a year.

37. Such as the Deutsche Pfandbriefanstalt. This is a mortgage bank, organized as a public law corporation, serving as an agency for public housing policy, and concerned with the financing of social housing.

38. *The Bulletin,* published by the Press and Information Office of the Federal German Government, Bonn, vol. 5, July 2, 1957.

39. *Wirtschaft und Statistik,* new series, vol. 10 (1957), pp. 4 and 174; *Rheinischer Merkur,* March 13, 1959.

40. See "Die Ausgaben von Bund, Ländern und Gemeinden zur Förderung des Wohnungsbaues in den Rechnungsjahren 1948 bis 1954," *Wirtschaft und Statistik,* new series, vol. 8 (1956), p. 374.

41. On financial administration and public finance generally, see the chapters by A. M. Hillhouse and Rodney L. Mott in Litchfield, *op. cit.,* chaps, 12 and 13.

42. Thus far, four federal transfer laws (Überleitungsgesetze) have been passed. The first dates from November 28, 1950 (*BGBl.,* 1950, pp. 773-777) and is still in force as amended.

43. "Revenues" is a broad term which includes a variety of intergovernmental transfers, some of which, such as equalization payments, will be discussed later.

44. For example, it was 31.7 percent in 1956. *Die Zeit,* March 20, 1958.

45. *New York Times,* July 4, 1958 and June 13, 1959.

46. Wilhelm Henle, "Finanzausgleich—die Schicksalfrage des Bundesstaates," *Politische Studien,* vol. 10 (1959), pp. 781-789, at p. 788.

47. To say nothing of differences among the military governors themselves!

48. On the negotiations concerning the financial articles,

130   THE STATES IN WEST GERMAN FEDERALISM

see Golay, *The Founding of the Federal Republic of Germany*, *op. cit.*, pp. 74-92.

49. *BGBl.*, 1955, I, p. 817; *ibid.*, 1956, I, p. 1077.

50. Article 108 on the collection machinery has been implemented by various federal statutes. See, for example, *BGBl.*, 1950, pp. 448-453; and *ibid.*, 1955, I, pp. 189-192. The collection machinery, which is partly federal, partly state and partly mixed, involves very complicated federal-state administrative arrangements. Thus the regional or intermediate finance offices (Oberfinanzdirektionen), created in 1950, are joint agencies; they are staffed partly by federal and partly by state personnel. The chief of each such office (Oberfinanzpräsident) is both a federal and a state official. This hybrid plan has met with German criticism. See Eschenburg, *Staat und Gesellschaft in Deutschland*, *op. cit.*, pp. 763-765.

51. *Die Finanzpolitik in der Wahlperiode 1953-1957*, Publication No. 50, Institut "Finanzen und Steuern" (Bonn, 1957), p. 53. The turnover tax is a sales tax on each transaction. Among the smaller sources of federal revenue were 710,300,000 DM from the alcoholic spirits monopoly, and 1,120,900,000 DM from fees and other administrative income.

52. The term "Finanzausgleich" dates back to legislation passed in the early days of the Weimar Republic. On the general problem involved, see Henle, "Finanzausgleich—die Schicksalfrage des Bundesstaates," *op. cit.*, pp. 781-789.

53. Vertical equalization may also refer to the division of revenues between state and local governments, or, in the most general sense, the division between federal, state and local units.

54. In 1959, the Federal Constitutional Court held unconstitutional a federal law (*BGBl.*, 1956, I, pp. 507-510) that required the states to bear expenditures which represented obligations of the Federal Government. *BVerfGE.*, vol. 9 (1959), pp. 305-334.

55. The Lastenausgleich funds are administered by a hybrid federal-state administrative setup directed by the independent Bundesausgleichsamt. While primarily intended as a scheme to equalize between individuals, it has some incidental effects in equalizing between states. In the fiscal year 1957, the Bund collected 1,190,000,000 DM from persons living in North Rhine–Westphalia and returned 890,000,000 DM to other persons living in that state. On the other hand, the Bund collected 101,000,000

DM from residents of Schleswig-Holstein and returned 228,-
000,000 DM to other residents of Schleswig-Holstein. *Der Städtetag,* new series, vol. 12 (1959), p. 216.

56. Statistisches Bundesamt, *Die öffentliche Finanzwirtschaft
in den Rechnungsjahren 1948 bis 1954* (Stuttgart, 1957), p. 82.

57. *Ibid.,* p. 71.

58. *BGBl.,* 1956, I, pp. 523-588.

59. Erstes Überleitungsgesetz in der Fassung von 28. April
1955, *BGBl.,* 1955, I, pp. 193 ff., section 21a.

60. For the dispute between the Germans of the Bonn Constitutional Convention and the Western Allies concerning the
wording of Article 106 of the Grundgesetz, see Golay, *The
Founding of the Federal Republic of Germany, op. cit.,* pp. 87-
92. Golay shows that Article 106-3 was an Allied-inspired clause
authorizing "federal grants-in-aid to the Länder on the American
model."

61. Arnold Köttgen, "Der Einfluss des Bundes auf die deutsche
Verwaltung und die Organisation der bundeseigenen Verwal-
tung," *Jahrbuch des öffentlichen Rechts der Gegenwart,* new
series, vol. 3 (Tübingen, 1954), pp. 67-147, at pp. 89, 90 and 93;
Henry P. Pilgert, *Community and Group Life in West Germany,*
Historical Division, Office of the U.S. High Commissioner for
Germany (Bad Godesberg, 1952), pp. 21-25.

62. The statistics in the above table are from the following
publications of the Statistisches Bundesamt. On per capita income, see "Das Sozialprodukt der Länder der Bundesrepublik
1950 bis 1955," *Wirtschaft und Statistik,* new series, vol. 9
(1957), pp. 595-600. On per capita yield of state and local taxes,
see *Die öffentliche Finanzwirtschaft in den Rechnungsjahren
1948 bis 1954, op. cit.,* p. 16.

63. Wilhelmine Dreissig, "Die finanz- und steuerpolitische
Entwicklung in der Bundesrepublik im Jahre 1954," *Finanzar-
chiv,* new series, vol. 16 (1955-1956), pp. 161-185, especially
"Der Finanzausgleich zwischen Bund und Länder," pp. 171-176.

64. *BGBl.,* 1959, I, pp. 73-76.

65. Although the Saar became a German Land on January 1,
1957, its economic union with the Federal Republic was not
formally completed until July 6, 1959.

66. The statistics are from the Zweite Verordnung zur Durch-
führung des Landerfinanzausgleichs im Ausgleichsjahr 1958,
BGBl., 1959, I, p. 649.

NOTES FOR CHAPTER FOUR

1. Heinrich Troeger as reported in the *Frankfurter Allgemeine Zeitung*, June 3, 1957.

2. August Dresbach writing in the same newspaper, March 23, 1957.

3. Karlheinz Neunreither, "Politics and Bureaucracy in the West German Bundesrat," *American Political Science Review*, vol. 53 (1959), pp. 713-731, at p. 717, footnote 14.

4. The first postwar conference of ministers-president was held in Bremen, October 4, 1956, on the invitation of Bürgermeister Wilhelm Kaisen and his cabinet. The ministers-president of the Soviet zone Länder did not appear and the French zone sent only unofficial observers. *Der Tagesspiegel* (Berlin), October 5, 1946. In 1945, the ministers-president of the U.S. zone were organized by military government into the Council of States (Länderrat). See Heinz Guradze, "The Länderrat: Landmark of German Reconstruction," *Western Political Quarterly*, vol. 3 (1950), pp. 190-213.

5. Hans Schäfer, *Der Bundesrat* (Cologne, 1955), pp. 31-32; and A. Koehler and K. Jansen, eds., *Die Bundesrepublik, 1958/59* (Berlin, 1958), *passim*.

6. *The Bulletin*, issued by the Press and Information Office of the German Federal Government, December 15, 1959; and Terence Prittie, "Eichmann and the Germans," *New Republic*, vol. 142, no. 22 (June 27, 1960), p. 8.

7. This number also includes some agreements between the Bund and one or more states. See Hans Schneider, "Staatsverträge und Verwaltungsabkommen zwischen deutschen Bundesländern," *Die öffentliche Verwaltung*, vol. 10 (1957), pp. 644-651.

8. For the text of the agreement, see Schleswig-Holstein, *GVBl.*, 1951, p. 59.

9. Subject to the transitional provisions of Article 132. On state "quotas" in the staffing of federal administrative agencies, see Article 36.

10. Otto Kirchheimer, "The Political Scene in West Germany," *World Politics*, vol. 9 (1957), pp. 433-445, at p. 444; and Theodor Eschenburg, "Ämterpatronage im Parteienstaat," *Politische Studien*, vol. 5 (1955), pp. 23-27.

11. On the reasons for the failure permanently to denazify the civil service, see Louis J. Edinger, "Post-Totalitarian Leadership:

Elites in the German Federal Republic," *American Political Science Review*, vol. 54 (1960), pp. 58-82, particularly p. 80.

12. *BGBl.*, 1951, I, pp. 307-322. See Georg Anders, *Kommentar zum Gesetz zur Regelung der Rechtsverhältnisse der unter Artikel 131 GG fallenden Personen* (4th ed., Stuttgart, 1959).

13. Taylor Cole, "Three Constitutional Courts," *American Political Science Review*, vol. 53 (1959), pp. 963-984, at pp. 979-980.

14. And also pay them 20 percent of their total salary expenditures. Failure to meet these requirements was to result in financial penalties payable to the Bund.

15. Karl Schultes, "German Politics and Political Theory," *Political Quarterly*, vol. 28 (1957), pp. 40-48, at p. 43.

16. The Federal Constitutional Court, in a 1954 decision, narrowly construed the scope of Rahmenvorschriften issued under Article 75-1. *BVerfGE.*, vol. 4 (1956), pp. 115-142.

17. *BGBl.*, 1955, I, pp. 477-488; Part II of this law contains the Rahmenvorschriften on "Personalvertretungen in den Ländern."

18. *BGBl.*, 1957, I, pp. 993-1045.

19. *BGBl.*, 1957, I, pp. 667-692.

20. Public personnel law and administration are discussed here solely from the standpoint of federal-state relations. No attempt is made to go into other aspects such as the distinction between officials (Beamte), employees (Angestellte) and workers (Arbeiter).

21. On federal coercion of states and emergency powers, see Articles 37 and 91. These are more carefully defined and safeguarded than was the case in the Weimar Constitution.

22. Diether Haas, "Bundesgesetze über Organisation und Verfahren der Landesbehörden," *Archiv des öffentlichen Rechts*, new series, vol. 41 (1955-1956), pp. 81-101, especially pp. 82-83.

23. Arnold Köttgen, *Die Gemeinde und der Bundesgesetzgeber* (Stuttgart, 1957), p. 62.

24. Bundesvertriebenengesetz, Article 21, *BGBl.*, 1953, I, pp. 201 ff. For a more extreme case, likewise involving refugees, in which federal law overrode state legislation on local government, see Kurt Held, "Der autonome Verwaltungsstil der Länder und das Bundesratsveto, nach Art. 84, Abs. 1 des Grundgesetzes," *Archiv des öffentlichen Rechts*, new series, vol. 41 (1955-1956), pp. 50-80, especially p. 76.

25. See, for example, Karl Josef Partsch, "Probleme der Schleswig-Holsteinischen Verwaltungsreform," *Der Städtetag,* new series, vol. 12 (1959), pp. 149-157; Wilhelm Henle, "Staatsvereinfachung in Bayern," *Die öffentliche Verwaltung,* vol. 10 (1957), pp. 273-277; and Fritz Rietdorf, "Das erste Vereinfachungsgesetz. Ein wichtiger Schritt auf dem Weg zur weiteren Verwaltungsreform in Nordrhein-Westfalen," *ibid.,* vol. 10 pp. 841-853.

26. See the newspaper comments on the reports of the Arbeitsgemeinschaft für Staatsvereinfachung in Bayern, *Frankfurter Allgemeine Zeitung* May 10, 1957; and *Rheinischer Merkur,* July 10, 1959.

27. Of the four states which do not have Regierungsbezirke (Bremen, Hamburg, the Saar, Schleswig-Holstein), only Schleswig-Holstein is large enough to justify such areas.

28. Many people in Land Lippe did not want their state swallowed up in North Rhine–Westphalia. As a sop to state pride, Lippe is treated as a separate Regierungsbezirk, as well as enjoying other concessions. A similar policy was followed in Lower Saxony with respect to the former states of Oldenburg and Brunswick. Both Oldenburg and Brunswick are Regierungsbezirke in fact but each has the special title of "Verwaltungsbezirk."

29. Herz has pointed out that, except in Bremen, Hamburg, and the Saar, the Länder have large administrative field staffs and that the central ministries at the state capital are relatively small. Gwendolen M. Carter, John H. Herz and John C. Ranney, *Major Foreign Powers. The Governments of Great Britain, France, Germany and the Soviet Union* (3d ed., New York, 1957), p. 477.

30. Horst Beuster, "Die Probleme der staatlichen Mittelinstanz," *Archiv des öffentlichen Rechts,* new series, vol. 39 (1952-1953), pp. 399-427; and *Die Mittelstufe der Verwaltung,* published by the Institut zur Förderung öffentlicher Angelegenheiten (Frankfurt, 1950).

31. See, for example, Hesse, Gesetz über die Mittelinstanz, *GVBl.,* 1953, pp. 93 ff.

32. The sphere of the states also includes concurrent power fields which the Bund has not yet pre-empted by legislation. Because of the large output of federal statutes dealing with concurrent matters, the state residuum has been greatly curtailed.

33. *BGBl.*, 1951, I, pp. 936-937, as amended by *BGBl.*, 1957, I, pp. 1058-1069.

34. Karl August Bettermann, "Bundeskompetenz für Jugendschutz?" *Archiv des öffentlichen Rechts,* new series, vol. 44 (1958), pp. 91-110.

35. Arthur J. Olsen, "Germans in Clash on Police Powers," *New York Times,* November 6, 1958.

36. Theodor Eschenburg, "Die Lücke in Schröders Entwurf," *Die Zeit,* January 29, 1960.

37. Local government fuctions are customarily divided into Selbstverwaltungsangelegenheiten and Auftragangelegenheiten. The former are the autonomous or self-governing functions which are exercised by local units under their own initiative and responsibility. The latter are mandatory functions delegated by the state to the local authorities and administered by them under state supervision. Matters relating to police traditionally fall within the second category.

38. See Robert M. W. Kempner, "Police Administration" in Edward H. Litchfield and Associates, *Governing Postwar Germany* (Ithaca, 1953), chap. 16.

39. Baden-Württemberg, Polizeigesetz, GB., 1955, pp. 249 ff.

40. *Der Städtetag,* new series, vol. 11 (1958), pp. 462-463.

41. See, for example, Fritz Rietdorf, "Die Grundsätze des neuen Nordrhein-Westfälischen Ordnungsbehördengesetzes," *Die öffentliche Verwaltung,* vol. 10 (1957), pp. 7-16.

42. On the history of the doctrine, see Heinrich Heffter, *Die deutsche Selbstverwaltung im 19. Jahrhundert* (Stuttgart, 1950).

43. Bremen, Hamburg, and West Berlin are city-states. There are 24,525 Gemeinden in West Germany, many of them with histories reaching back through the centuries. *Statistisches Jahrbuch für die Bundesrepublik Deutschland, 1959,* p. 37.

44. The Stadtkreis is "kreisfrei" instead of "kreisangehörig." There were 136 Stadtkreise in West Germany in 1958, *op. cit.,* pp. 29-35.

45. For a study of the intergovernmental relations between counties and their kreisangehörige cities, see Fredo Wagener, *Die Städte im Landkreis* (Göttingen, 1955).

46. Heffter, *Die deutsche Selbstverwaltung im 19. Jahrhundert, op. cit., passim.* There are 425 Landkreise in the Federal Republic.

47. Siedlungsverband Ruhrkohlenbezirk. See Peter Seydel, *Die kommunalen Zweckverbände* (Göttingen, 1955); and Roger H. Wells, *German Cities* (Princeton, 1932), pp. 187-194.

48. See Willi Kreiterling, "La Rhenanie du Nord-Westphalie," in Alfred Grosser, ed., *Administration et politique en Allemagne occidentale* (Paris, 1954), pp. 116-128.

49. They are discussed in other works. See Hans Peters, ed., *Handbuch der kommunalen Wissenschaft und Praxis* (3 vols., Berlin, 1956-1959); Rudolf Elleringmann, *Grundlagen der Kommunalverfassung und der Kommunalaufsicht* (Stuttgart, 1957); and Richard Hiscocks, *Democracy in Western Germany* (London, 1957), chap. 8. See also the writer's "Local Government" in Litchfield, *op. cit.*, chap. 3 and his article in the *National Municipal Review*, vol. 45 (1956), pp. 66-71.

50. For the texts of the Gemeindeordnungen, see Wilhelm Loschelder, ed., *Die Gemeindeordnungen in den westdeutschen Ländern und die Verfassungen von Berlin, Hamburg und Bremen* (2d ed., Stuttgart, 1956).

51. *Die Zeit*, March 20, 1958. For the text of the Landkreisordnung, see Lower Saxony, *GVBl.*, 1958, pp. 17 ff.

52. See A. Koehler and K. Jansen, eds., *Die Bundesrepublik, 1958/59* (Berlin, 1958), *passim;* Litchfield, *op. cit.*, pp. 79-81; and Roger H. Wells, "The Revival of German Unions of Local Authorities after World War II," *American Political Science Review*, vol. 41 (1947), pp. 1182-1187.

53. Otto Ziebill, *Geschichte des Deutschen Städtetages. Fünfzig Jahre deutsche Kommunalpolitik* (2d ed., Stuttgart, 1956).

54. *Die Landkreise in der Bundesrepublik. Zehn Jahre Aufbauarbeit,* published under the auspices of the Deutscher Landkreistag (Stuttgart, 1955).

55. Arnold Köttgen, *Die Gemeinde und der Bundesgesetzgeber* (Stuttgart, 1957), p. 11. In 1957, some 75 federal laws and ordinances were enacted which had direct effects upon the Gemeinden and Gemeindeverbände. *Der Städtetag*, new series, vol. 11 (1958), p. 374. It is not surprising that one of the standing committees of the Bundestag is the "Ausschuss für Kommunalpolitik und öffentliche Fürsorge." *Amtliches Handbuch des Deutschen Bundestages. 3. Wahlperiode* (Darmstadt, 1958), p. 173. From the *Handbuch,* the writer computed that 239 out of the 519 Bundestag members had had, since 1945, experience

in local legislatures or in local offices such as Bürgermeister or Landrat.

56. Köttgen, *op. cit.*, p. 97. The Bund also makes contractual agreements with particular local governments but these are almost always of a private law rather than of a public law character. *Ibid.*, p. 19.

57. *Ibid.*, pp. 77-78.

58. *BGBl.*, 1957, I, pp. 1696-1702. See also *Der Städtetag*, new series, vol. 11 (1958), p. 374.

59. Otto Ziebill, "Kommunalpolitik in unserer Zeit," *ibid.*, vol. 11 (1958), pp. 341-345.

60. *Ibid.*, vol. 12 (1959), p. 216.

61. Herbert Sattler, "Zum kommunalen Finanzsystem," *ibid.*, vol. 10 (1957), pp. 495-498; "Verbesserung der kommunalen Finanzen. Memorandum der Bundesvereinigung der Kommunalen Spitzenverbände," *ibid.*, vol. 11 (1958), pp. 289-293; and Erwin Hielscher, "Gemeindefinanzen seit 1945," *Die öffentliche Verwaltung*, vol. 12 (1959), pp. 409-413.

62. *Der Städtetag*, vol. 13 (1960), p. 67.

63. Johannes Popitz, *Der künftige Finanzausgleich zwischen Reich, Ländern und Gemeinden* (Berlin, 1932), p. 89.

64. *Der Städtetag*, new series, vol. 11 (1958), p. 293.

65. *BGBl.*, 1955, I, pp. 817 ff.; *BGBl.*, 1956, I, pp. 1077 ff. On Land legislation amending the state finance equalization laws so as to provide for the local percentage of the income and corporation tax yield, see *Der Städtetag*, vol. 10 (1957), p. 1; *ibid.*, vol. 11 (1958), p. 373. For example, in the case of Hesse, it was fixed at 18.5.

66. Article 106-7 has some resemblance to legislation passed by the United States Congress authorizing federal aid to public schools in "federally affected areas."

67. Important federal statutes were passed in 1960 such as the Strassenbaufinanzierungsgesetz, *BGBl.*, 1960, I, pp. 201-205; and the Bundesbaugesetz, *ibid.*, pp. 341-388. The interest of the cities in such legislation, especially in its financial implications, is understandable. See "Gemeindepfenning," *Der Städtetag*, vol. 13 (1960), pp. 155-156.

NOTES FOR CHAPTER FIVE

1. Article 75-2 is discussed in connection with mass communications media. In passing, it may be mentioned that one of the standing committees of the Bundestag is the Ausschuss für Kulturpolitik und Publizistik. *Amtliches Handbuch des Deutschen Bundestages. 3. Wahlperiode, op. cit.,* p. 173.

2. *The Bulletin,* published by the Press and Information Office of the German Federal Government, September 10, 1957.

3. *Die Bundesrepublik Deutschland, 1958/59, op. cit., passim.*

4. In their conference at Munich in February 1954, the ministers-president of the Länder objected to this federal ministry's use of funds for cultural purposes. They argued that it is for the states alone to determine the necessity of such expenditures. *Die Gegenwart,* vol. 9 (1954), p. 102.

5. See Hans Wallenberg, *Report on Democratic Institutions in Germany* (New York, 1956), pp. 19-24.

6. The controversies over mass communications media and education will be discussed under those headings. An interesting borderline dispute may be mentioned here without, however, going into details. The case involved the transfer of certain cultural property of the former state of Prussia. In 1957, over the objection of the Bundesrat, the Bundestag passed a law creating the foundation, "Preussischer Kulturbesitz." *BGBl.,* 1957, I, pp. 841-843. In 1959, the Federal Constitutional Court upheld the constitutionality of the law. *BVerfGE.,* vol. 10 (1960), pp. 21-55.

7. The above discussion deals only incidentally with federal-state relations in respect to motion pictures. Here, in the years from 1949 to 1953, the Bund played a more active role than it now does. This was because questions of industrial decartelization and deconcentration were involved, subjects which fall within the concurrent legislative jurisdiction of the federation. See Henry P. Pilgert, *Press, Radio and Film in West Germany, 1945-1953,* Historical Division, Office of the U.S. High Commissioner for Germany (Bad Godesberg, 1953); and Paul Heimann, "Das deutsche Filmwesen der Gegenwart," *Universitas* (German edition), vol. 14 (1959), pp. 395-405.

8. W. Phillips Davison, "The Mass Media in West German Political Life," in Hans Speier and W. Phillips Davison, eds.,

West German Leadership and Foreign Policy (Evanston, Illinois, 1957) , chap. 7; Frede Castberg, *Freedom of Speech in the West: A Comparative Study of Public Law in France, the United States and Germany* (New York, 1960); and Peter J. Fliess, "Freedom of the Press in the Bonn Republic," *Journal of Politics,* vol. 16 (1954), pp. 664-684.

9. Harold Zink, *The United States in Germany, 1944-1955* (Princeton, 1957), chap. 15; and Pilgert, *op. cit.*

10. "Bonn stellt Pressegesetz-Entwurf zur öffentlichen Diskussion," *Die Neue Zeitung,* March 13, 1952; and Claus Jacobi, "The New German Press," *Foreign Affairs,* vol. 32 (1953-1954), pp. 323-330, at p. 330.

11. "New Control Plan is Revived in Bonn," *New York Times,* Feburary 7, 1957.

12. *BGBl.,* 1953, I, pp. 377 ff.

13. A recent case (1959-1960) involved the German translation (*Die Rechnung ohne den Wirt*) of James M. Cain's well-known crime novel, *The Postman Always Rings Twice.* Banned as dangerous to youth under the law of 1953, the publisher took the case to the courts. He lost in the lower court but the appellate court "temporarily set aside the ban." See Paul Hühnerfeld, "Anatomie eines (literarischen) Mordes. Angeklagt: Die Bundesrepublik Deutschland, vertreten durch die Bundesprüfstelle für Jugendgefährdendes Schrifttum," *Die Zeit,* July 1, 1960.

14. Adapted from Pilgert, *op. cit.,* p. 23.

15. *BVerfGE.,* vol. 7 (1958), pp. 29-45.

16. *Official Gazette of the Allied High Commission for Germany,* No. 1, September 23, 1949, p. 7.

17. And also the legislation relating to radio.

18. In 1959, a Hamburg court enjoined the distribution of an issue of West Germany's widely read illustrated magazine, *Der Stern.* The prohibited number contained an alleged libelous article entitled, "Who Protects Us from the Office for the Protection of the Constitution?" *New York Times,* February 19, 1959.

19. Speier and Davison, *op. cit.;* Pilgert, *op. cit.*

20. *Lex cit.*

21. Radio Free Berlin is not to be confused with RIAS ("Radio in the American Sector" of Berlin), established and operated under United States Government auspices since 1946.

22. For the text of the treaty as ratified by the Schleswig-Holstein Landtag see *GVBl.*, 1955, pp. 17 ff.

23. North Rhine–Westphalia, *GVBl.*, 1955, pp. 195 ff.

24. *Frankfurter Allgemeine Zeitung*, February 7, 1959. The over-all organization of the broadcasting corporations is the Arbeitsgemeinschaft der öffentlich-rechtlich Rundfunkanstalten der Bundesrepublik. *Die Bundesrepublik, 1958/59, op. cit.*, p. 320.

25. *The Bulletin*, published by the Press and Information Office of the German Federal Government, July 15, 1958; *U.S. News and World Report*, vol. 47, November 23, 1959, p. 52.

26. *New York Times*, November 8, 1959.

27. *Ibid.*, November 13, 1959.

28. See Robert T. Holt, *Radio Free Europe* (Minneapolis, 1958).

29. *Rheinischer Merkur*, July 17, 1959; *New York Times*, July 17, 1960.

30. "Ein Vorschlag zur Funk-Ordnung," *Die Zeit*, August 1, 1957.

31. *Frankfurter Allgemeine Zeitung*, March 21, 1959.

32. *Ibid.*, May 30, 1959.

33. *New York Times*, November 14, 1959. The bill also called forth Soviet protests because it was proposed to locate the administrative headquarters of the new setup in West Berlin. *U.S. Department of State Bulletin*, vol. 42 (No. 1071, January 4, 1960), pp. 7-8. Adenauer's latest proposal for a television corporation organized under private law has met with even greater protest. *New York Times*, July 27, 1960; *Die Zeit*, July 22 and 29, 1960.

34. Henry P. Pilgert, *The West German Educational System*, Historical Division, Office of the U.S. High Commissioner for Germany (Bad Godesberg, 1953); Wallenberg, *Report on Democratic Institutions in Germany, op. cit.*, chap. 7; Alina Lindegren, *Germany Revisited: Education in the Federal Republic*, U.S. Department of Health, Education and Welfare (Washington, 1957); and Theodor Maunz, "Staat und Schule in Verfassung und Wirklichkeit," *Politische Studien*, vol. 10 (1959), pp. 497-507.

35. Hans Heckel, "Die deutsche Schule in Zahlen," *Frankfurter Hefte*, vol. 13 (1958), pp. 237-244, at p. 239.

36. E. Krause, "Vocational Training in the Federal Republic

of Germany," *International Labour Review,* vol. 77 (1958) pp. 209-219.

37. Hellmut Becker, "Erwachsenenbildung in der Bundesrepublik. Das Gutachten des Deutschen Ausschusses für Erziehungs- und Bildungswesen," *Die Zeit,* April 8, 1960; and Alice Hanson Cook, *Adult Education in Citizenship in Postwar Germany* (Pasadena, 1954). On political education in general, see Hiscocks, *Democracy in Western Germany, op. cit.,* chap. 12; and Thomas Ellwein, *Pflegt die deutsche Schule Bürgerbewusstsein?* (Munich, 1955).

38. Rüdiger Robert Beer, "Zwischen Bildung und Ausbildung," *Der Städtetag,* new series, vol. 10 (1957), pp. 385-388.

39. Friedrich Edding, *Internationale Tendenzen in der Entwicklung der Ausgaben für Schulen und Hochschulen,* published by the Institut für Weltwirtschaft in Kiel, as cited in *Frankfurter Hefte,* vol. 14 (1959), p. 496.

40. *Die Zeit,* January 23, 1958.

41. "Kulturpolitik—zu leicht gemacht," *ibid.,* February 6, 1958. Cultural autonomy is intimately connected with religious differences, as the struggle over confessional schools (discussed below) so well shows.

42. It is appropriate that the defense of federalism should be made by a minister of a state which has taken the lead in school reform. One of the values of federalism in education is that it permits the more progressive Länder to pioneer.

43. See also Articles 2, 5, 6, 11, 12.

44. Hans Schuster, "Bildungspolitik im Bundesstaat," *Politische Studien,* vol. 11 (1960), pp. 449-459, at pp. 451-452.

45. *Frankfurter Allgemeine Zeitung,* July 24, 1959.

46. Theodor Eschenburg, who in general defends the present pattern of federal-state legislative and administrative relations, criticizes the lack of federal authority to to enact Rahmengesetze in the field of education. See his *Staat und Gesellschaft in Deutschland, op. cit.,* pp. 763-765.

47. For the controversy between ASTA and the Rector and Senate of the University of Freiburg, see "Studenten-Rebellion in Freiburg," *Die Zeit,* July 22, 1960.

48. Biermann-Ratjen, *op. cit.* Agreements between the Länder in the field of education had also been used in the Weimar Republic but not as extensively as in the Bundesrepublik.

49. Abkommen zwischen den Ländern der Bundesrepublik zur Vereinheitlichung auf dem Gebiete des Schulwesens.

50. For the text of the 1954 resolution, see Johannes Hohlfeld, ed., *Dokumente der Deutschen Politik und Geschichte,* vol. 8 (Berlin, 1955), pp. 339-340.

51. "Die Länge der Sommerferien bleibt offen," *Frankfurter Allgemeine Zeitung,* February 14, 1959.

52. Sydney Gruson, "West Berlin Asks History Revision," *New York Times,* January 13, 1960; Robert Strobel, "Wird der Geschichtsunterricht besser?" *Die Zeit,* January 15, 1960; and Helmut Hirsch, "Geschichtsunterricht in der Volksschule," *Frankfurter Hefte,* vol. 15 (1960), pp. 413-416.

53. Hans Bohnenkamp, "Gesamtplan für die deutsche Schule," *Frankfurter Hefte,* vol. 14 (1959), pp. 315-326; and "Vorschlag für einen neuen Schulaufbau," *Frankfurter Allgemeine Zeitung,* April 18, 1959. For the text of the plan, see "Das Gutachten zur Schulreform," *Das Parlament,* vol. 9 (1959), pp. 5-10.

54. Walter Dirks, "Der sicherste Weg zum Bundeskultusministerium. Oder: Jeder Land sein eigener Rahmenplan," *Frankfurter Hefte,* vol. 14 (1959), pp. 543-545. Dirks attacks the counterproposal to the Committee report, made by the Rhineland-Palatinate Ministry of Education.

55. From time to time, current developments in school legislation are reported in *Der Städtetag.* See, for example, Dietrich Oedekoven, "Neue Schulgesetze in den Ländern der Bundesrepublik," *ibid.,* new series, vol. 11 (1958), pp. 408-410.

56. Alexander Kluge, *Die Universitätsselbstverwaltung. Ihre Geschichte und gegenwärtige Rechtsform* (Frankfurt, 1958).

57. Hans Heckel, "Die deutsche Schule in Zahlen," *op. cit.,* p. 240. See also Hans Heckel, *Die Städte und ihre Schulen. Leistung und Bedeutung der Städte für die Entwicklung und den Bestand des deutschen Schulwesens* (Stuttgart, 1959).

58. Heckel, "Die deutsche Schule in Zahlen," *op. cit.,* p. 244.

59. Erwin Stein, "Elterliche Mitbeteiligung im deutschen Schulwesen," *Juristenzeitung,* vol. 12 (1957), pp. 11-17.

60. "Eine Fünf in Verfassungstreue?" *Die Zeit,* February 6, 1958; and Friedrich Minssen, "Schulbehörden, Lehrerschaft und Elternbeiräte vor den Problemen der Schulreform. Aus der Praxis in Hessen," *Frankfurter Hefte,* vol. 14 (1959), pp. 483-496. However, it should be noted that Article 56-6 of the Hesse

Constitution is unique among the West German Landesverfassungen.

61. Baden-Württemberg, Article 8; Bavaria, Article 182; North
Rhine–Westphalia, Article 23.

62. In North Rhine–Westphalia, Schleswig-Holstein and
Lower Saxony. See the Vertrag of Lower Saxony with the
Evangelical Landeskirchen which was ratified by the Landtag,
April 18, 1955. *GVBl.*, 1955, pp. 159 ff.

63. For a fuller discussion of these questions, see Roger H.
Wells, "The Financial Relations of Church and State in Germany, 1919-1937," *Political Science Quarterly,* vol. 53 (1938),
pp. 36-59. The church taxes are compulsory and can be avoided
only by formal withdrawal from church membership.

64. *Statistisches Jahrbuch für die Bundesrepublik Deutschland, 1957,* p. 45.

65. In 1956, the Evangelical Landeskirchen had 26,700,000
members and the Catholic Church, 24,501,238. These statistics
include the Saar but not West Berlin. *Ibid., 1959,* p. 76.

66. See Thomas Ellwein, *Klerikalismus in der deutschen
Politik* (Munich, 1955). This controversial book provoked many
replies. See *Kritikspiegel zu Band I: Klerikalismus in der deutschen Politik* (Munich, 1956).

67. Frank Eyck, "Tensions in Western Germany," *Contemporary Review,* vol. 191 (1957), pp. 325-328, at p. 325. For a
case of "Konfessionsarithmetik" involving the office of school
superintendent in the city of Bonn, see "Des Schulrats falsches
Gesangbuch," *Die Zeit,* February 6, 1958. When a county public
hospital advertised for a Catholic physician, Theodor Eschenburg promptly criticized the action as violating Articles 3-3 and
33-3 of the Grundgesetz. See "Verfassungswidriges Stellen-In-
serat," *ibid.,* March 11, 1960.

68. During the campaign which preceded the 1957 Bundestag
election, a group of pastors and laymen in the Evangelical
Church of Württemberg sharply protested against the use of
the name "Christian" by any political party. Focko Lüpsen,
"Religion Confuses German Election," *Christian Century,* vol.
74 (1957), p. 996.

69. On the historical background of the question, see Ernst
Christian Helmreich, *Religious Education in German Schools.
An Historical Approach* (Cambridge, Mass., 1959).

70. A federal law of 1921 gave children who had reached the age of fifteen the right to make their own decisions about religious instruction. *RGBl.,* 1921, I, pp. 939-941. This is still the rule in the West German states except in Bavaria and Rhineland-Palatinate where the age is eighteen years.

71. There was a similar provision in the Weimar Constitution, Article 149.

72. "Erziehungsberechtigte" is literally translated "upon the request of those entitled to education," but it really means "upon the request of parents and other persons responsible for the education of children." Since the Reich law mentioned in Article 146-2 was never enacted, Article 174 preserved the status quo in the states.

73. Helmreich *op. cit.,* p. 137.

74. *Statistisches Jahrbuch für die Bundesrepublik Deutschland, 1956,* p. 79. The statistics do not include Lower Saxony. The writer was unable to obtain more recent statistics.

75. "Katholische Grundsätze über die Erziehungs- und Schulwesen," reprinted in Johannes Hohlfeld, ed., *Dokumente der Deutschen Politik und Geschichte,* vol. 6 (Berlin, 1952), pp. 257-260. Not only must Catholic children be taught by Catholic teachers in Catholic elementary public schools, but the teachers must also be trained in Catholic public teacher training institutions. In other words, the teachers' colleges must also be "Bekenntnisschulen."

76. "Episcopat und 'Rahmenplan,'" *Rheinischer Merkur,* July 10, 1959.

77. According to the Evangelical Church of Hesse and Nassau. See "Landeskirche gegen Konfessionsschule," *Die Neue Zeitung,* February 25, 1953; and "Niemöller über rheinhessischen Schulstreit," *ibid.,* April 14, 1953.

78. Statistics as quoted by Ellwein, *op. cit.,* pp 138-139, from the official publications of the Bavarian Statistisches Landesamt.

79. Rhineland-Palatinate, *GVBl.,* 1955, pp. 1 ff.

80. Bavaria, *GVBl.,* 1958, pp. 133 ff. See also Ellwein, *op. cit.,* pp. 212-244.

81. Gesetz über das öffentliche Schulwesen in Niedersachsen, *GVBl.,* 1954, pp. 89 ff. Relevant excerpts from the law are given in Hohlfeld, *op. cit.,* vol. 8, pp. 422-428. Hohlfeld also reprints the joint pastoral letter of the Roman Catholic bishops, protesting against the bill, and the address of Minister-President

Kopf defending it. *Ibid.*, pp. 415-422. For details on the controversy, see Ellwein, *op. cit.*, pp. 183-212.

82. Werner Weber, "Die Verfassung Niedersachsens," *Archiv des öffentlichen Rechts,* new series, vol. 38 (1951-1952), pp. 362-364. For a somewhat analogous provision, see Article 89 of the Constitution of North Rhine–Westphalia on the school system of the former Land Lippe.

83. As a temporary measure, British military government revived the principle of the 1906 act, subject to local referendum. In effect, this enabled Bekenntnisschulen to be established after the fall of the Hitler regime.

84. Not counting Oldenburg, 2,876 of the 4,051 Volksschulen in Lower Saxony were in this category.

85. Helmreich, *op. cit.,* p. 232.

86. *BVerfGE.,* vol. 6 (1957), pp. 309-367.

87. See Hans Kohn, "Out of Catastrophe: Germany 1945-1960," *Review of Politics,* vol. 22 (1960), pp. 163-174. The writer is in full agreement with the views set forth by Professor Kohn's article. For a more critical analysis, see Karl W. Deutsch and Lewis J. Edinger, "Germany Rejoins the Powers," *Yale Review,* vol. 49 (1959-1960), pp. 20-42.

INDEX

DATE DUE

MAY 1 3			
JAN 1 8			
AUG 7			
JUL 2 5			
GAYLORD			PRINTED IN U.S.A.